Diary of a Pilgrimage

Diary of a Pilgrimage

Jerome K. Jerome

MINT EDITIONS

Diary of a Pilgrimage was first published in 1891.

This edition published by Mint Editions 2021.

ISBN 9781513278506 | E-ISBN 9781513278964

Published by Mint Editions®

MINT
EDITIONS

minteditionbooks.com

Publishing Director: Jennifer Newens
Design & Production: Rachel Lopez Metzger
Project Manager: Micaela Clark
Typesetting: Westchester Publishing Services

Monday, 19th

My friend B. called on me this morning and asked me if I would go to a theatre with him on Monday next.

"Oh, yes! certainly, old man," I replied. "Have you got an order, then?" He said:

"No; they don't give orders. We shall have to pay."

"Pay! Pay to go into a theatre!" I answered, in astonishment. "Oh, nonsense! You are joking."

"My dear fellow," he rejoined, "do you think I should suggest paying if it were possible to get in by any other means? But the people who run this theatre would not even understand what was meant by a 'free list,' the uncivilised barbarians! It is of no use pretending to them that you are on the Press, because they don't want the Press; they don't think anything of the Press. It is no good writing to the acting manager, because there is no acting manager. It would be a waste of time offering to exhibit bills, because they don't have any bills—not of that sort. If you want to go in to see the show, you've got to pay. If you don't pay, you stop outside; that's their brutal rule."

"Dear me," I said, "what a very unpleasant arrangement! And whereabouts is this extraordinary theatre? I don't think I can ever have been inside it."

"I don't think you have," he replied; "it is at Ober-Ammergau—first turning on the left after you leave Ober railway-station, fifty miles from Munich."

"Um! rather out of the way for a theatre," I said. "I should not have thought an outlying house like that could have afforded to give itself airs."

"The house holds seven thousand people," answered my friend B., "and money is turned away at each performance. The first production is on Monday next. Will you come?"

I pondered for a moment, looked at my diary, and saw that Aunt Emma was coming to spend Saturday to Wednesday next with us, calculated that if I went I should miss her, and might not see her again for years, and decided that I would go.

To tell the truth, it was the journey more than the play that tempted me. To be a great traveller has always been one of my cherished ambitions. I yearn to be able to write in this sort of strain:—

"I have smoked my fragrant Havana in the sunny streets of old Madrid, and I have puffed the rude and not sweet-smelling calumet of peace in the draughty wigwam of the Wild West; I have sipped my evening coffee in the silent tent, while the tethered camel browsed without upon the desert grass, and I have quaffed the fiery brandy of the North while the reindeer munched his fodder beside me in the hut, and the pale light of the midnight sun threw the shadows of the pines across the snow; I have felt the stab of lustrous eyes that, ghostlike, looked at me from out veil-covered faces in Byzantium's narrow ways, and I have laughed back (though it was wrong of me to do so) at the saucy, wanton glances of the black-eyed girls of Jedo; I have wandered where 'good'—but not too good—Haroun Alraschid crept disguised at nightfall, with his faithful Mesrour by his side; I have stood upon the bridge where Dante watched the sainted Beatrice pass by; I have floated on the waters that once bore the barge of Cleopatra; I have stood where Caesar fell; I have heard the soft rustle of rich, rare robes in the drawing-rooms of Mayfair, and I have heard the teeth-necklaces rattle around the ebony throats of the belles of Tongataboo; I have panted beneath the sun's fierce rays in India, and frozen under the icy blasts of Greenland; I have mingled with the teeming hordes of old Cathay, and, deep in the great pine forests of the Western World, I have lain, wrapped in my blanket, a thousand miles beyond the shores of human life."

B., to whom I explained my leaning towards this style of diction, said that exactly the same effect could be produced by writing about places quite handy. He said:—

"I could go on like that without having been outside England at all. I should say:

"I have smoked my fourpenny shag in the sanded bars of Fleet Street, and I have puffed my twopenny Manilla in the gilded balls of the Criterion; I have quaffed my foaming beer of Burton where Islington's famed Angel gathers the little thirsty ones beneath her shadowing wings, and I have sipped my tenpenny *ordinaire* in many a garlic-scented salon of Soho. On the back of the strangely-moving ass I have urged—or, to speak more correctly, the proprietor of the ass, or his agent, from behind has urged—my wild career across the sandy heaths of Hampstead, and my canoe has startled the screaming wild-fowl from their lonely haunts amid the sub-tropical regions of Battersea. Adown the long, steep slope of One Tree Hill have I rolled from top to foot, while laughing maidens of the East stood round and clapped their hands and yelled; and, in the old-world garden of that pleasant Court, where played the fair-haired children of the ill-starred Stuarts, have I wandered long through many paths, my arm entwined about the waist of one of Eve's sweet daughters, while her mother raged around indignantly on the other side of the hedge, and never seemed to get any nearer to us. I have chased the lodging-house Norfolk Howard to his watery death by the pale lamp's light; I have, shivering, followed the leaping flea o'er many a mile of pillow and sheet, by the great Atlantic's margin. Round and round, till the heart—and not only the heart—grows sick, and the mad brain whirls and reels, have I ridden the small, but extremely hard, horse, that may, for a penny, be mounted amid the plains of Peckham Rye; and high above the heads of the giddy throngs of Barnet (though it is doubtful if anyone among them was half so giddy as was I) have I swung in highly-coloured car, worked by a man with a rope. I have trod in stately measure the floor of Kensington's Town Hall (the tickets were a guinea each, and included refreshments—when you could get to them through the crowd), and on the green sward of the forest that borders eastern Anglia by the oft-sung town of Epping I have performed quaint ceremonies in a ring; I have mingled with the teeming hordes of Drury Lane on Boxing Night, and, during the run of a high-class piece, I have sat in lonely grandeur in the front row of the gallery, and wished that I had spent my shilling instead in the Oriental halls of the Alhambra."

"There you are," said B., "that is just as good as yours; and you can write like that without going more than a few hours' journey from London."

"We will discuss the matter no further," I replied. "You cannot, I see, enter into my feelings. The wild heart of the traveller does not throb within your breast; you cannot understand his longings. No matter! Suffice it that I will come this journey with you. I will buy a German conversation book, and a check-suit, and a blue veil, and a white umbrella, and suchlike necessities of the English tourist in Germany, this very afternoon. When do you start?"

"Well," he said, "it is a good two days' journey. I propose to start on Friday."

"Is not Friday rather an unlucky day to start on?" I suggested.

"Oh, good gracious!" he retorted quite sharply, "what rubbish next? As if the affairs of Europe were going to be arranged by Providence according to whether you and I start for an excursion on a Thursday or a Friday!"

He said he was surprised that a man who could be so sensible, occasionally, as myself, could have patience to even think of such old-womanish nonsense. He said that years ago, when he was a silly boy, he used to pay attention to this foolish superstition himself, and would never upon any consideration start for a trip upon a Friday.

But, one year, he was compelled to do so. It was a case of either starting on a Friday or not going at all, and he determined to chance it.

He went, prepared for and expecting a series of accidents and misfortunes. To return home alive was the only bit of pleasure he hoped for from that trip.

As it turned out, however, he had never had a more enjoyable holiday in his life before. The whole event was a tremendous success.

And after that, he had made up his mind to *always* start on a Friday; and he always did, and always had a good time.

He said that he would never, upon any consideration, start for a trip upon any other day but a Friday now. It was so absurd, this superstition about Friday.

So we agreed to start on the Friday, and I am to meet him at Victoria Station at a quarter to eight in the evening.

Thursday, 22nd

The Question of Luggage.—First Friend's Suggestion.—
Second Friend's Suggestion.—Third Friend's Suggestion.—
Mrs. Briggs' Advice.—Our Vicar's Advice.—His Wife's
Advice.—Medical Advice.—Literary Advice.—George's
Recommendation.—My Sister-in-Law's Help.—Young Smith's
Counsel.—My Own Ideas.—B.'s Idea.

I have been a good deal worried to-day about the question of what
luggage to take with me. I met a man this morning, and he said:

"Oh, if you are going to Ober-Ammergau, mind you take plenty of
warm clothing with you. You'll need all your winter things up there."

He said that a friend of his had gone up there some years ago, and
had not taken enough warm things with him, and had caught a chill
there, and had come home and died. He said:

"You be guided by me, and take plenty of warm things with you."

I met another man later on, and he said:

"I hear you are going abroad. Now, tell me, what part of Europe are
you going to?"

I replied that I thought it was somewhere about the middle. He
said:

"Well, now, you take my advice, and get a calico suit and a sunshade.
Never mind the look of the thing. You be comfortable. You've no idea of
the heat on the Continent at this time of the year. English people will
persist in travelling about the Continent in the same stuffy clothes that
they wear at home. That's how so many of them get sunstrokes, and are
ruined for life."

I went into the club, and there I met a friend of mine—a newspaper
correspondent—who has travelled a good deal, and knows Europe
pretty well. I told him what my two other friends had said, and asked
him which I was to believe. He said:

"Well, as a matter of fact, they are both right. You see, up in those
hilly districts, the weather changes very quickly. In the morning it may
be blazing hot, and you will be melting, and in the evening you may be
very glad of a flannel shirt and a fur coat."

"Why, that is exactly the sort of weather we have in England!" I
exclaimed. "If that's all these foreigners can manage in their own country,

what right have they to come over here, as they do, and grumble about our weather?"

"Well, as a matter of fact," he replied, "they haven't any right; but you can't stop them—they will do it. No, you take my advice, and be prepared for everything. Take a cool suit and some thin things, for if it's hot, and plenty of warm things in case it is cold."

When I got home I found Mrs. Briggs there, she having looked in to see how the baby was. She said:—

"Oh! if you're going anywhere near Germany, you take a bit of soap with you."

She said that Mr. Briggs had been called over to Germany once in a hurry, on business, and had forgotten to take a piece of soap with him, and didn't know enough German to ask for any when he got over there, and didn't see any to ask for even if he had known, and was away for three weeks, and wasn't able to wash himself all the time, and came home so dirty that they didn't know him, and mistook him for the man that was to come to see what was the matter with the kitchen boiler.

Mrs. Briggs also advised me to take some towels with me, as they give you such small towels to wipe on.

I went out after lunch, and met our Vicar. He said:

"Take a blanket with you."

He said that not only did the German hotel-keepers never give you sufficient bedclothes to keep you warm of a night, but they never properly aired their sheets. He said that a young friend of his had gone for a tour through Germany once, and had slept in a damp bed, and had caught rheumatic fever, and had come home and died.

His wife joined us at this point. (He was waiting for her outside a draper's shop when I met him.) He explained to her that I was going to Germany, and she said:

"Oh! take a pillow with you. They don't give you any pillows—not like our pillows—and it's *so* wretched, you'll never get a decent night's rest if you don't take a pillow." She said: "You can have a little bag made for it, and it doesn't look anything."

I met our doctor a few yards further on. He said:

"Don't forget to take a bottle of brandy with you. It doesn't take up much room, and, if you're not used to German cooking, you'll find it handy in the night."

He added that the brandy you get at foreign hotels was mere poison, and that it was really unsafe to travel abroad without a bottle of brandy.

He said that a simple thing like a bottle of brandy in your bag might often save your life.

Coming home, I ran against a literary friend of mine. He said:

"You'll have a goodish time in the train old fellow. Are you used to long railway journeys?"

I said:

"Well, I've travelled down from London into the very heart of Surrey by a South Eastern express."

"Oh! that's a mere nothing, compared with what you've got before you now," he answered. "Look here, I'll tell you a very good idea of how to pass the time. You take a chessboard with you and a set of men. You'll thank me for telling you that!"

George dropped in during the evening. He said:

"I'll tell you one thing you'll have to take with you, old man, and that's a box of cigars and some tobacco."

He said that the German cigar—the better class of German cigar— was of the brand that is technically known over here as the "Penny Pickwick—Spring Crop;" and he thought that I should not have time, during the short stay I contemplated making in the country, to acquire a taste for its flavour.

My sister-in-law came in later on in the evening (she is a thoughtful girl), and brought a box with her about the size of a tea-chest. She said:

"Now, you slip that in your bag; you'll be glad of that. There's everything there for making yourself a cup of tea."

She said that they did not understand tea in Germany, but that with that I should be independent of them.

She opened the case, and explained its contents to me. It certainly was a wonderfully complete arrangement. It contained a little caddy full of tea, a little bottle of milk, a box of sugar, a bottle of methylated spirit, a box of butter, and a tin of biscuits: also, a stove, a kettle, a teapot, two cups, two saucers, two plates, two knives, and two spoons. If there had only been a bed in it, one need not have bothered about hotels at all.

Young Smith, the Secretary of our Photographic Club, called at nine to ask me to take him a negative of the statue of the dying Gladiator in the Munich Sculpture Gallery. I told him that I should be delighted to oblige him, but that I did not intend to take my camera with me.

"Not take your camera!" he said. "You are going to Germany—to Rhineland! You are going to pass through some of the most picturesque scenery, and stay at some of the most ancient and famous towns of

Europe, and are going to leave your photographic apparatus behind you, and you call yourself an artist!"

He said I should never regret a thing more in my life than going without that camera.

I think it is always right to take other people's advice in matters where they know more than you do. It is the experience of those who have gone before that makes the way smooth for those who follow. So, after supper, I got together the things I had been advised to take with me, and arranged them on the bed, adding a few articles I had thought of all by myself.

I put up plenty of writing paper and a bottle of ink, along with a dictionary and a few other books of reference, in case I should feel inclined to do any work while I was away. I always like to be prepared for work; one never knows when one may feel inclined for it. Sometimes, when I have been away, and have forgotten to bring any paper and pens and ink with me, I have felt so inclined for writing; and it has quite upset me that, in consequence of not having brought any paper and pens and ink with me, I have been unable to sit down and do a lot of work, but have been compelled, instead, to lounge about all day with my hands in my pockets.

Accordingly, I always take plenty of paper and pens and ink with me now, wherever I go, so that when the desire for work comes to me I need not check it.

That this craving for work should have troubled me so often, when I had no paper, pens, and ink by me, and that it never, by any chance, visits me now, when I am careful to be in a position to gratify it, is a matter over which I have often puzzled.

But when it does come I shall be ready for it.

I also put on the bed a few volumes of Goethe, because I thought it would be so pleasant to read him in his own country. And I decided to take a sponge, together with a small portable bath, because a cold bath is so refreshing the first thing in the morning.

B. came in just as I had got everything into a pile. He stared at the bed, and asked me what I was doing. I told him I was packing.

"Great Heavens!" he exclaimed. "I thought you were moving! What do you think we are going to do—camp out?"

"No!" I replied. "But these are the things I have been advised to take with me. What is the use of people giving you advice if you don't take it?"

He said:

"Oh! take as much advice as you like; that always comes in useful to give away. But, for goodness sake, don't get carrying all that stuff about with you. People will take us for Gipsies."

I said:

"Now, it's no use your talking nonsense. Half the things on this bed are life-preserving things. If people go into Germany without these things, they come home and die."

And I related to him what the doctor and the vicar and the other people had told me, and explained to him how my life depended upon my taking brandy and blankets and sunshades and plenty of warm clothing with me.

He is a man utterly indifferent to danger and risk—incurred by other people—is B. He said:

"Oh, rubbish! You're not the sort that catches a cold and dies young. You leave that co-operative stores of yours at home, and pack up a tooth-brush, a comb, a pair of socks, and a shirt. That's all you'll want."

I HAVE PACKED MORE THAN that, but not much. At all events, I have got everything into one small bag. I should like to have taken that tea arrangement—it would have done so nicely to play at shop with in the train!—but B. would not hear of it.

I hope the weather does not change.

Friday, 23rd

Early Rising.—Ballast should be Stowed Away in the Hold before Putting to Sea.—Annoying Interference of Providence in Matters that it Does Not Understand.—A Socialistic Society.—B. Misjudges Me.—An Uninteresting Anecdote.—We Lay in Ballast.—A Moderate Sailor.—A Playful Boat.

I got up very early this morning. I do not know why I got up early. We do not start till eight o'clock this evening. But I don't regret it—the getting up early I mean. It is a change. I got everybody else up too, and we all had breakfast at seven.

I made a very good lunch. One of those seafaring men said to me once:

"Now, if ever you are going a short passage, and are at all nervous, you lay in a good load. It's a good load in the hold what steadies the ship. It's them half-empty cruisers as goes a-rollin' and a-pitchin' and a-heavin' all over the place, with their stern up'ards half the time. You lay in ballast."

It seemed very reasonable advice.

Aunt Emma came in the afternoon. She said she was so glad she had caught me. Something told her to change her mind and come on Friday instead of Saturday. It was Providence, she said.

I wish Providence would mind its own business, and not interfere in my affairs: it does not understand them.

She says she shall stop till I come back, as she wants to see me again before she goes. I told her I might not be back for a month. She said it didn't matter; she had plenty of time, and would wait for me.

The family entreat me to hurry home.

I ate a very fair dinner—"laid in a good stock of ballast," as my seafaring friend would have said; wished "Good-bye!" to everybody, and kissed Aunt Emma; promised to take care of myself—a promise which, please Heaven, I will faithfully keep, cost me what it may—hailed a cab and started.

I reached Victoria some time before B. I secured two corner seats in a smoking-carriage, and then paced up and down the platform waiting for him.

When men have nothing else to occupy their minds, they take to thinking. Having nothing better to do until B. arrived, I fell to musing.

What a wonderful piece of Socialism modern civilisation has become!—not the Socialism of the so-called Socialists—a system modelled apparently upon the methods of the convict prison—a system under which each miserable sinner is to be compelled to labour, like a beast of burden, for no personal benefit to himself, but only for the good of the community—a world where there are to be no men, but only numbers—where there is to be no ambition and no hope and no fear,—but the Socialism of free men, working side by side in the common workshop, each one for the wage to which his skill and energy entitle him; the Socialism of responsible, thinking individuals, not of State-directed automata.

Here was I, in exchange for the result of some of my labour, going to be taken by Society for a treat, to the middle of Europe and back. Railway lines had been laid over the whole 700 or 800 miles to facilitate my progress; bridges had been built, and tunnels made; an army of engineers, and guards, and signal-men, and porters, and clerks were waiting to take charge of me, and to see to my comfort and safety. All I had to do was to tell Society (here represented by a railway booking-clerk) where I wanted to go, and to step into a carriage; all the rest would be done for me. Books and papers had been written and printed; so that if I wished to beguile the journey by reading, I could do so. At various places on the route, thoughtful Society had taken care to be ready for me with all kinds of refreshment (her sandwiches might be a little fresher, but maybe she thinks new bread injurious for me). When I am tired of travelling and want to rest, I find Society waiting for me with dinner and a comfortable bed, with hot and cold water to wash in and towels to wipe upon. Wherever I go, whatever I need, Society, like the enslaved genii of some Eastern tale, is ready and anxious to help me, to serve me, to do my bidding, to give me enjoyment and pleasure. Society will take me to Ober-Ammergau, will provide for all my wants on the way, and, when I am there, will show me the Passion Play, which she has arranged and rehearsed and will play for my instruction; will bring me back any way I like to come, explaining, by means of her guide-books and histories, everything upon the way that she thinks can interest me; will, while I am absent, carry my messages to those I have left behind me in England, and will bring me theirs in return; will look after me and take care of me and protect me like a mother—as no mother ever could.

All that she asks in return is, that I shall do the work she has given me to do. As a man works, so Society deals by him.

To me Society says: "You sit at your desk and write, that is all I want you to do. You are not good for much, but you can spin out yards of what you and your friends, I suppose, call literature; and some people seem to enjoy reading it. Very well: you sit there and write this literature, or whatever it is, and keep your mind fixed on that. I will see to everything else for you. I will provide you with writing materials, and books of wit and humour, and paste and scissors, and everything else that may be necessary to you in your trade; and I will feed you and clothe you and lodge you, and I will take you about to places that you wish to go to; and I will see that you have plenty of tobacco and all other things practicable that you may desire—provided that you work well. The more work you do, and the better work you do, the better I shall look after you. You write—that is all I want you to do."

"But," I say to Society, "I don't like work; I don't want to work. Why should I be a slave and work?"

"All right," answers Society, "don't work. I'm not forcing you. All I say is, that if you don't work for me, I shall not work for you. No work from you, no dinner from me—no holidays, no tobacco."

And I decide to be a slave, and work.

Society has no notion of paying all men equally. Her great object is to encourage brain. The man who merely works by his muscles she regards as very little superior to the horse or the ox, and provides for him just a little better. But the moment he begins to use his head, and from the labourer rises to the artisan, she begins to raise his wages.

Of course hers is a very imperfect method of encouraging thought. She is of the world, and takes a worldly standard of cleverness. To the shallow, showy writer, I fear, she generally pays far more than to the deep and brilliant thinker; and clever roguery seems often more to her liking than honest worth. But her scheme is a right and sound one; her aims and intentions are clear; her methods, on the whole, work fairly well; and every year she grows in judgment.

One day she will arrive at perfect wisdom, and will pay each man according to his deserts.

But do not be alarmed. This will not happen in our time.

Turning round, while still musing about Society, I ran against B.

(literally). He thought I was a clumsy ass at first, and said so; but, on recognising me, apologised for his mistake. He had been there for some time also, waiting for me. I told him that I had secured two corner seats in a smoking-carriage, and he replied that he had done so too. By a curious coincidence, we had both fixed upon the same carriage. I had taken the corner seats near the platform, and he had booked the two opposite corners. Four other passengers sat huddled up in the middle. We kept the seats near the door, and gave the other two away. One should always practise generosity.

There was a very talkative man in our carriage. I never came across a man with such a fund of utterly uninteresting anecdotes. He had a friend with him—at all events, the man was his friend when they started—and he talked to this friend incessantly, from the moment the train left Victoria until it arrived at Dover. First of all he told him a long story about a dog. There was no point in the story whatever. It was simply a bald narrative of the dog's daily doings. The dog got up in the morning and barked at the door, and when they came down and opened the door there he was, and he stopped all day in the garden; and when his wife (not the dog's wife, the wife of the man who was telling the story) went out in the afternoon, he was asleep on the grass, and they brought him into the house, and he played with the children, and in the evening he slept in the coal-shed, and next morning there he was again. And so on, for about forty minutes.

A very dear chum or near relative of the dog's might doubtless have found the account enthralling; but what possible interest a stranger—a man who evidently didn't even know the dog—could be expected to take in the report, it was difficult to conceive.

The friend at first tried to feel excited, and murmured: "Wonderful!" "Very strange, indeed!" "How curious!" and helped the tale along by such exclamations as, "No, did he though?" "And what did you do then?" or, "Was that on the Monday or the Tuesday, then?" But as the story progressed, he appeared to take a positive dislike to the dog, and only yawned each time that it was mentioned.

Indeed, towards the end, I think, though I trust I am mistaken, I heard him mutter, "Oh, damn the dog!"

After the dog story, we thought we were going to have a little quiet. But we were mistaken; for, with the same breath with which he finished the dog rigmarole, our talkative companion added:

"But I can tell you a funnier thing than that—"

We all felt we could believe that assertion. If he had boasted that he could tell a duller, more uninteresting story, we should have doubted him; but the possibility of his being able to relate something funnier, we could readily grasp.

But it was not a bit funnier, after all. It was only longer and more involved. It was the history of a man who grew his own celery; and then, later on, it turned out that his wife was the niece, by the mother's side, of a man who had made an ottoman out of an old packing-case.

The friend glanced round the carriage apologetically about the middle of this story, with an expression that said:

"I'm awfully sorry, gentlemen; but it really is not my fault. You see the position I'm in. Don't blame me. Don't make it worse for me to bear than it is."

And we each replied with pitying, sympathetic looks that implied:

"That's all right, my dear sir; don't you fret about that. We see how it is. We only wish we could do something to help you."

The poor fellow seemed happier and more resigned after that.

B. and I hurried on board at Dover, and were just in time to secure the last two berths in the boat; and we were glad that we had managed to do this because our idea was that we should, after a good supper, turn in and go comfortably to sleep.

B. said:

"What I like to do, during a sea passage, is to go to sleep, and then wake up and find that I am there."

We made a very creditable supper. I explained to B. the ballast principle held by my seafaring friend, and he agreed with me that the idea seemed reasonable; and, as there was a fixed price for supper, and you had as much as you liked, we determined to give the plan a fair trial.

B. left me after supper somewhat abruptly, as it appeared to me, and I took a stroll on deck by myself. I did not feel very comfortable. I am what I call a moderate sailor. I do not go to excess in either direction. On ordinary occasions, I can swagger about and smoke my pipe, and lie about my Channel experiences with the best of them. But when there is what the captain calls "a bit of a sea on," I feel sad, and try to get away from the smell of the engines and the proximity of people who smoke green cigars.

There was a man smoking a peculiarly mellow and unctuous cigar on deck when I got there. I don't believe he smoked it because he enjoyed it. He did not look as if he enjoyed it. I believe he smoked it merely to show how well he was feeling, and to irritate people who were not feeling very well.

There is something very blatantly offensive about the man who feels well on board a boat.

I am very objectionable myself, I know, when I am feeling all right. It is not enough for me that I am not ill. I want everybody to see that I am not ill. It seems to me that I am wasting myself if I don't let every human being in the vessel know that I am not ill. I cannot sit still and be thankful, like you'd imagine a sensible man would. I walk about the ship—smoking, of course—and look at people who are not well with mild but pitying surprise, as if I wondered what it was like and how they did it. It is very foolish of me, I know, but I cannot help it. I suppose it is the human nature that exists in even the best of us that makes us act like this.

I could not get away from this man's cigar; or when I did, I came within range of the perfume from the engine-room, and felt I wanted to go back to the cigar. There seemed to be no neutral ground between the two.

If it had not been that I had paid for saloon, I should have gone fore. It was much fresher there, and I should have been much happier there altogether. But I was not going to pay for first-class and then ride third—that was not business. No, I would stick to the swagger part of the ship, and feel aristocratic and sick.

A mate, or a boatswain, or an admiral, or one of those sort of people—I could not be sure, in the darkness, which it was—came up to me as I was leaning with my head against the paddle-box, and asked me what I thought of the ship. He said she was a new boat, and that this was her first voyage.

I said I hoped she would get a bit steadier as she grew older.

He replied: "Yes, she is a bit skittish to-night."

What it seemed to me was, that the ship would try to lie down and go to sleep on her right side; and then, before she had given that position a fair trial, would suddenly change her mind, and think she could do it better on her left. At the moment the man came up to me she was trying to stand on her head; and before he had finished speaking she had given up this attempt, in which, however, she had very nearly succeeded, and had, apparently, decided to now play at getting out of the water altogether.

And this is what he called being a "bit skittish!"

Seafaring people talk like this, because they are silly, and do not know any better. It is no use being angry with them.

I got a little sleep at last. Not in the bunk I had been at such pains to secure: I would not have stopped down in that stuffy saloon, if anybody had offered me a hundred pounds for doing so. Not that anybody did; nor that anybody seemed to want me there at all. I gathered this from the fact that the first thing that met my eye, after I had succeeded in clawing my way down, was a boot. The air was full of boots. There were sixty men sleeping there—or, as regards the majority, I should say *trying* to sleep there—some in bunks, some on tables, and some under tables. One man *was* asleep, and was snoring like a hippopotamus— like a hippopotamus that had caught a cold, and was hoarse; and the other fifty-nine were sitting up, throwing their boots at him. It was a snore, very difficult to locate. From which particular berth, in that dimly-lighted, evil-smelling place, it proceeded nobody was quite sure. At one moment, it appeared to come, wailing and sobbing, from the larboard, and the next instant it thundered forth, seemingly from the starboard. So every man who could reach a boot picked it up, and threw it promiscuously, silently praying to Providence, as he did so, to guide it aright and bring it safe to its desired haven.

I watched the weird scene for a minute or two, and then I hauled myself on deck again, and sat down—and went to sleep on a coil of rope; and was awakened, in the course of time, by a sailor who wanted that coil of rope to throw at the head of a man who was standing, doing no harm to anybody, on the quay at Ostend.

JEROME K. JEROME

SATURDAY, 24TH

ARRIVAL AT OSTEND.—COFFEE AND ROLLS.—DIFFICULTY OF
MAKING FRENCH WAITERS UNDERSTAND GERMAN.—ADVANTAGES
OF POSSESSING A CONSCIENCE THAT DOES NOT GET UP TOO
EARLY.—VILLAINY TRIUMPHANT.—VIRTUE ORDERED OUTSIDE.—A
HOMELY ENGLISH ROW.

When I say I was "awakened" at Ostend, I do not speak the strict truth. I was not awakened—not properly. I was only half-awakened. I never did get fairly awake until the afternoon. During the journey from Ostend to Cologne I was three-parts asleep and one-part partially awake.

At Ostend, however, I was sufficiently aroused to grasp the idea that we had got somewhere, and that I must find my luggage and B., and do something or other; in addition to which, a strange, vague instinct, but one which I have never yet known deceive me, hovering about my mind, and telling me that I was in the neighbourhood of something to eat and drink, spurred me to vigour and action.

I hurried down into the saloon and there found B. He excused himself for having left me alone all night—he need not have troubled himself. I had not pined for him in the least. If the only woman I had ever loved had been on board, I should have sat silent, and let any other fellow talk to her that wanted to, and that felt equal to it—by explaining that he had met a friend and that they had been talking. It appeared to have been a trying conversation.

I also ran against the talkative man and his companion. Such a complete wreck of a once strong man as the latter looked I have never before seen. Mere sea-sickness, however severe, could never have accounted for the change in his appearance since, happy and hopeful, he entered the railway-carriage at Victoria six short hours ago. His friend, on the other hand, appeared fresh and cheerful, and was relating an anecdote about a cow.

We took our bags into the Custom House and opened them, and I sat down on mine, and immediately went to sleep.

When I awoke, somebody whom I mistook at first for a Field-Marshal, and from force of habit—I was once a volunteer—saluted, was standing over me, pointing melodramatically at my bag. I assured him in picturesque German that I had nothing to declare. He did not appear to comprehend me, which struck me as curious, and took the bag away from me, which left me nothing to sit upon but the floor. But I felt too sleepy to be indignant.

After our luggage had been examined, we went into the buffet. My instinct had not misled me: there I found hot coffee, and rolls and butter. I ordered two coffees with milk, some bread, and some butter. I ordered them in the best German I knew. As nobody understood me, I went and got the things for myself. It saves a deal of argument, that method. People seem to know what you mean in a moment then.

B. suggested that while we were in Belgium, where everybody spoke French, while very few indeed knew German, I should stand a better chance of being understood if I talked less German and more French.

He said:

"It will be easier for you, and less of a strain upon the natives. You stick to French," he continued, "as long as ever you can. You will get along much better with French. You will come across people now and then—smart, intelligent people—who will partially understand your French, but no human being, except a thought-reader, will ever obtain any glimmering of what you mean from your German."

"Oh, are we in Belgium," I replied sleepily; "I thought we were in Germany. I didn't know." And then, in a burst of confidence, I added, feeling that further deceit was useless, "I don't know where I am, you know."

"No, I thought you didn't," he replied. "That is exactly the idea you give anybody. I wish you'd wake up a bit."

We waited about an hour at Ostend, while our train was made up. There was only one carriage labelled for Cologne, and four more passengers wanted to go there than the compartment would hold.

Not being aware of this, B. and I made no haste to secure places, and, in consequence, when, having finished our coffee, we leisurely strolled up and opened the carriage door we saw that every seat was already booked. A bag was in one space and a rug in another, an umbrella booked a third, and so on. Nobody was there, but the seats were gone!

It is the unwritten law among travellers that a man's luggage deposited upon a seat, shall secure that seat to him until he comes to sit upon it himself. This is a good law and a just law, and one that, in my normal state, I myself would die to uphold and maintain.

But at three o'clock on a chilly morning one's moral sensibilities are not properly developed. The average man's conscience does not begin work till eight or nine o'clock—not till after breakfast, in fact. At three A.M. he will do things that at three in the afternoon his soul would revolt at.

Under ordinary circumstances I should as soon have thought of shifting a man's bag and appropriating his seat as an ancient Hebrew squatter would have thought of removing his neighbour's landmark; but at this time in the morning my better nature was asleep.

I have often read of a man's better nature being suddenly awakened. The business is generally accomplished by an organ-grinder or a little child (I would back the latter, at all events—give it a fair chance—to awaken anything in this world that was not stone deaf, or that had not been dead for more than twenty-four hours); and if an organ-grinder or a little child had been around Ostend station that morning, things might have been different.

B. and I might have been saved from crime. Just as we were in the middle of our villainy, the organ-grinder or the child would have struck up, and we should have burst into tears, and have rushed from the carriage, and have fallen upon each other's necks outside on the platform, and have wept, and waited for the next train.

As it was, after looking carefully round to see that nobody was watching us, we slipped quickly into the carriage, and, making room for ourselves among the luggage there, sat down and tried to look innocent and easy.

B. said that the best thing we could do, when the other people came, would be to pretend to be dead asleep, and too stupid to understand anything.

I replied that as far as I was concerned, I thought I could convey the desired impression without stooping to deceit at all, and prepared to make myself comfortable.

A few seconds later another man got into the carriage. He also made room for himself among the luggage and sat down.

"I am afraid that seat's taken, sir," said B. when he had recovered his surprise at the man's coolness. "In fact, all the seats in this carriage are taken."

"I can't help that," replied the ruffian, cynically. "I've got to get to Cologne some time to-day, and there seems no other way of doing it that I can see."

"Yes, but so has the gentleman whose seat you have taken got to get there," I remonstrated; "what about him? You are thinking only of yourself!"

My sense of right and justice was beginning to assert itself, and I felt quite indignant with the fellow. Two minutes ago, as I have explained, I could contemplate the taking of another man's seat with equanimity. Now, such an act seemed to me shameful. The truth is that my better nature never sleeps for long. Leave it alone and it wakens of its own accord. Heaven help me! I am a sinful, worldly man, I know; but there is good at the bottom of me. It wants hauling up, but it's there.

This man had aroused it. I now saw the sinfulness of taking another passenger's place in a railway-carriage.

But I could not make the other man see it. I felt that some service was due from me to Justice, in compensation of the wrong I had done her a few moments ago, and I argued most eloquently.

My rhetoric was, however, quite thrown away. "Oh! it's only a vice-consul," he said; "here's his name on the bag. There's plenty of room for him in with the guard."

It was no use my defending the sacred cause of Right before a man who held sentiments like that; so, having lodged a protest against his behaviour, and thus eased my conscience, I leant back and dozed the doze of the just.

Five minutes before the train started, the rightful owners of the carriage came up and crowded in. They seemed surprised at finding only five vacant seats available between seven of them, and commenced to quarrel vigorously among themselves.

B. and I and the unjust man in the corner tried to calm them, but passion ran too high at first for the voice of Reason to be heard. Each combination of five, possible among them, accused each remaining two of endeavouring to obtain seats by fraud, and each one more than hinted that the other six were liars.

What annoyed me was that they quarrelled in English. They all had languages of their own,—there were four Belgians, two Frenchmen, and a German,—but no language was good enough for them to insult each other in but English.

Finding that there seemed to be no chance of their ever agreeing among themselves, they appealed to us. We unhesitatingly decided in favour of the five thinnest, who, thereupon, evidently regarding the matter as finally settled, sat down, and told the other two to get out.

These two stout ones, however—the German and one of the Belgians—seemed inclined to dispute the award, and called up the station-master.

The station-master did not wait to listen to what they had to say, but at once began abusing them for being in the carriage at all. He told them they ought to be ashamed of themselves for forcing their way into a compartment that was already more than full, and inconveniencing the people already there.

He also used English to explain this to them, and they got out on the platform and answered him back in English.

English seems to be the popular language for quarrelling in, among foreigners. I suppose they find it more expressive.

We all watched the group from the window. We were amused and interested. In the middle of the argument an early gendarme arrived on the scene. The gendarme naturally supported the station-master. One man in uniform always supports another man in uniform, no matter what the row is about, or who may be in the right—that does not trouble him. It is a fixed tenet of belief among uniform circles that a uniform can do no wrong. If burglars wore uniform, the police would be instructed to render them every assistance in their power, and to take into custody any householder attempting to interfere with them in the execution of their business. The gendarme assisted the station-master to abuse the two stout passengers, and he also abused them in English. It was not good English in any sense of the word. The man would probably have been able to give his feelings much greater variety and play in French or Flemish, but that was not his object. His ambition, like every other foreigner's, was to become an accomplished English quarreller, and this was practice for him.

A Customs House clerk came out and joined in the babel. He took the part of the passengers, and abused the station-master and the gendarme, and *he* abused *them* in English.

B. said he thought it very pleasant here, far from our native shores, in the land of the stranger, to come across a little homely English row like this.

A MAN OF FAMILY.—AN ECCENTRIC TRAIN.—OUTRAGE ON AN
ENGLISHMAN.—ALONE IN EUROPE.—DIFFICULTY OF MAKING
GERMAN WAITERS UNDERSTAND SCANDINAVIAN.—DANGER OF
KNOWING TOO MANY LANGUAGES.—A WEARISOME JOURNEY.—
COLOGNE, AHOY!

There was a very well-informed Belgian in the carriage, and he told us something interesting about nearly every town through which we passed. I felt that if I could have kept awake, and have listened to that man, and remembered what he said, and not mixed things up, I should have learnt a good deal about the country between Ostend and Cologne.

He had relations in nearly every town, had this man. I suppose there have been, and are, families as large and as extensive as his; but I never heard of any other family that made such a show. They seemed to have been planted out with great judgment, and were now all over the country. Every time I awoke, I caught some such scattered remark as:

"Bruges—you can see the belfry from this side—plays a polka by Haydn every hour. My aunt lives here." "Ghent—Hotel de Ville, some say finest specimen of Gothic architecture in Europe—where my mother lives. You could see the house if that church wasn't there." "Just passed Alost—great hop centre. My grandfather used to live there; he's dead now." "There's the Royal chateau—here, just on this side. My sister is married to a man who lives there—not in the palace, I don't mean, but in Laeken." "That's the dome of the Palais de Justice—they call Brussels 'Paris in little'—I like it better than Paris, myself—not so crowded. I live in Brussels." "Louvain—there's Van de Weyer's statue, the 1830 revolutionist. My wife's mother lives in Louvain. She wants us to come and live there. She says we are too far away from her at Brussels, but I don't think so." "Leige—see the citadel? Got some cousins at Leige—only second ones. Most of my first ones live at Maestricht"; and so on all the way to Cologne.

I do not believe we passed a single town or village that did not possess one or more specimens of this man's relatives. Our journey seemed, not so much like a tour through Belgium and part of Northern Germany, as a visit to the neighbourhood where this man's family resided.

I was careful to take a seat facing the engine at Ostend. I prefer to travel that way. But when I awoke a little later on, I found myself going backwards.

I naturally felt indignant. I said:

"Who's put me over here? I was over there, you know. You've no right to do that!"

They assured me, however, that nobody had shifted me, but that the train had turned round at Ghent.

I was annoyed at this. It seemed to me a mean trick for a train to start off in one direction, and thus lure you into taking your seat (or somebody else's seat, as the case might be) under the impression that you were going to travel that way, and then, afterwards, turn round and go the other way. I felt very doubtful, in my own mind, as to whether the train knew where it was going at all.

At Brussels we got out and had some more coffee and rolls. I forget what language I talked at Brussels, but nobody understood me. When I next awoke, after leaving Brussels, I found myself going forwards again. The engine had apparently changed its mind for the second time, and was pulling the carriages the other way now. I began to get thoroughly alarmed. This train was simply doing what it liked. There was no reliance to be placed upon it whatever. The next thing it would do would be to go sideways. It seemed to me that I ought to get up and see into this matter; but, while pondering the business, I fell asleep again.

I was very sleepy indeed when they routed us out at Herbesthal, to examine our luggage for Germany. I had a vague idea that we were travelling in Turkey, and had been stopped by brigands. When they told me to open my bag, I said, "Never!" and remarked that I was an Englishman, and that they had better be careful. I also told them that they could dismiss any idea of ransom from their minds at once, unless they were prepared to take I.O.U.'s, as it was against the principles of our family to pay cash for anything—certainly not for relatives.

They took no notice of my warning, and caught hold of my Gladstone. I resisted feebly, but was over-powered, and went to sleep again.

On awakening, I discovered myself in the buffet. I have no recollection of going there. My instinct must have guided me there during my sleep.

I ordered my usual repast of coffee and rolls. (I must have been full of coffee and rolls by this time.) I had got the idea into my head now that I was in Norway, and so I ordered them in broken Scandinavian, a few words of which I had picked up during a trip through the fiords last summer.

Of course, the man did not understand; but I am accustomed to witnessing the confusion of foreigners when addressed in their native tongue, and so forgave him—especially as, the victuals being well within reach, language was a matter of secondary importance.

I took two cups of coffee, as usual—one for B., and one for myself—and, bringing them to the table, looked round for B. I could not see him anywhere. What had become of him? I had not seen him, that I could recollect, for hours. I did not know where I was, or what I was doing. I had a hazy knowledge that B. and I had started off together—whether yesterday or six months ago, I could not have said to save my life—with the intention, if I was not mistaken, of going somewhere and seeing something. We were now somewhere abroad—somewhere in Norway was my idea; though why I had fixed on Norway is a mystery to me to this day—and I had lost him!

How on earth were we ever to find each other again? A horrible picture presented itself to my mind of our both wandering distractedly up and down Europe, perhaps for years, vainly seeking each other. The touching story of Evangeline recurred to me with terrible vividness.

Something must be done, and that immediately. Somehow or another I must find B. I roused myself, and summoned to my aid every word of Scandinavian that I knew.

It was no good these people pretending that they did not understand their own language, and putting me off that way. They had got to understand it this time. This was no mere question of coffee and rolls; this was a serious business. I would make that waiter understand my Scandinavian, if I had to hammer it into his head with his own coffee-pot!

I seized him by the arm, and, in Scandinavian that must have been quite pathetic in its tragic fervour, I asked him if he had seen my friend—my friend B.

The man only stared.

I grew desperate. I shook him. I said:

"My friend—big, great, tall, large—is he where? Have you him to see where? Here?"

(I had to put it that way because Scandinavian grammar is not a strong point with me, and my knowledge of the verbs is as yet limited to the present tense of the infinitive mood. Besides, this was no time to worry about grace of style.)

JEROME K. JEROME

A crowd gathered round us, attracted by the man's terrified expression. I appealed to them generally. I said:

"My friend B.—head, red—boots, yellow, brown, gold—coat, little squares—nose, much, large! Is he where? Him to see—anybody—where?"

Not a soul moved a hand to help me. There they stood and gaped!

I repeated it all over again louder, in case anybody on the outskirts of the mob had not heard it; and I repeated it in an entirely new accent. I gave them every chance I could.

They chatted excitedly among themselves, and, then a bright idea seemed to strike one of them, a little more intelligent-looking than the rest, and he rushed outside and began running up and down, calling out something very loudly, in which the word "Norwegian" kept on occurring.

He returned in a few seconds, evidently exceedingly pleased with himself, accompanied by a kindly-looking old gentleman in a white hat.

Way was made in the crowd, and the old gentleman pressed forward. When he got near, he smiled at me, and then proceeded to address to me a lengthy, but no doubt kindly meant, speech in Scandinavian.

Of course, it was all utterly unintelligible to me from beginning to end, and my face clearly showed this. I can grasp a word or two of Scandinavian here and there, if pronounced slowly and distinctly; but that is all.

The old gentleman regarded me with great surprise. He said (in Scandinavian, of course):

"You speak Norwegian?"

I replied, in the same tongue:

"A little, a very little—*very*."

He seemed not only disappointed, but indignant. He explained the matter to the crowd, and they all seemed indignant.

Why everybody should be indignant with me I could not comprehend. There are plenty of people who do not understand Scandinavian. It was absurd to be vexed with me because *I* did not. I do know a little, and that is more than some people do.

I inquired of the old gentleman about B. He did understand me. I must give him credit for that. But beyond understanding me, he was of no more use than the others; and why they had taken so much trouble to fetch him, I could not imagine.

What would have happened if the difficulty had continued much longer (for I was getting thoroughly wild with the lot of them) I cannot say. Fortunately, at this moment I caught sight of B. himself, who had just entered the room.

I could not have greeted him more heartily if I had wanted to borrow money of him.

"Well, I *am* glad to see you again!" I cried. "Well, this *is* pleasant! I thought I had lost you!"

"Why, you are English!" cried out the old gentleman in the white hat, in very good Saxon, on hearing me speak to B.

"Well, I know that," I replied, "and I'm proud of it. Have you any objection to my being English?"

"Not in the least," he answered, "if you'd only talk English instead of Norwegian. I'm English myself;" and he walked away, evidently much puzzled.

B. said to me as we sat down:

"I'll tell you what's the matter with you, J.—you know too many languages for this continent. Your linguistic powers will be the ruin of us if you don't hold them in a bit. You don't know any Sanscrit or Chaldean, do you?"

I replied that I did not.

"Any Hebrew or Chinese?"

"Not a word."

"Sure?"

"Not so much as a full stop in any of them."

"That's a blessing," said B., much relieved. "You would be trying to palm off one or other of them on some simple-minded peasant for German, if you did!"

It is a wearisome journey, through the long, hot hours of the morning, to Cologne. The carriage is stifling. Railway travellers, I have always noticed, regard fresh air as poison. They like to live on the refuse of each other's breath, and close up every window and ventilator tight. The sun pours down through glass and blind and scorches our limbs. Our heads and our bodies ache. The dust and soot drift in and settle on our clothes, and grime our hands and face. We all doze and wake up with a start, and fall to sleep again upon each other. I wake, and find my neighbour with his head upon my shoulder. It seems a shame to cast him off; he looks so trustful. But he is heavy. I push him on to the man the other side. He is just as happy there. We roll about; and when the train jerks, we butt each other with our heads. Things fall from the rack upon us. We look up surprised, and go to sleep again. My bag tumbles down upon the head of the unjust man in the corner. (Is it retribution?) He starts up, begs my pardon, and sinks back into oblivion. I am too sleepy to pick up the bag. It lies there on the floor. The unjust man uses it for a footstool.

We look out, through half-closed eyes, upon the parched, level, treeless land; upon the little patchwork farms of corn and beetroot, oats and fruit, growing undivided, side by side, each looking like a little garden dropped down into the plain; upon the little dull stone houses.

A steeple appears far away upon the horizon. (The first thing that we ask of men is their faith: "What do you believe?" The first thing that they show us is their church: "*This* we believe.") Then a tall chimney ranges itself alongside. (First faith, then works.) Then a confused jumble of roofs, out of which, at last, stand forth individual houses, factories, streets, and we draw up in a sleeping town.

People open the carriage door, and look in upon us. They do not appear to think much of us, and close the door again quickly, with a bang, and we sleep once more.

As we rumble on, the country slowly wakes. Rude V-shaped carts, drawn by yoked oxen, and even sometimes by cows, wait patiently while we cross the long, straight roads stretching bare for many a mile across the plain. Peasants trudge along the fields to work. Smoke rises from the villages and farm-houses. Passengers are waiting at the wayside stations.

Towards mid-day, on looking out, we see two tiny spires standing side by side against the sky. They seem to be twins, and grow taller as we approach. I describe them to B., and he says they are the steeples of Cologne Cathedral; and we all begin to yawn and stretch, and to collect our bags and coats and umbrellas.

Half of Saturday 24th, and Some of Sunday, 25th

Difficulty of Keeping this Diary.—A Big Wash.—The German Bed.—Its Goings On.—Manners and Customs of the German Army.—B.'s Besetting Sin.—Cologne Cathedral.—Thoughts Without Words.—A Curious Custom.

This diary is getting mixed. The truth is, I am not living as a man who keeps a diary should live. I ought, of course, to sit down in front of this diary at eleven o'clock at night, and write down all that has occurred to me during the day. But at eleven o'clock at night, I am in the middle of a long railway journey, or have just got up, or am just going to bed for a couple of hours. We go to bed at odd moments, when we happen to come across a bed, and have a few minutes to spare. We have been to bed this afternoon, and are now having another breakfast; and I am not quite sure whether it is yesterday or to-morrow, or what day it is.

I shall not attempt to write up this diary in the orthodox manner, therefore; but shall fix in a few lines whenever I have half-an-hour with nothing better to do.

We washed ourselves in the Rhine at Cologne (we had not had a wash since we had left our happy home in England). We started with the idea of washing ourselves at the hotel; but on seeing the basin and water and towel provided, I decided not to waste my time playing with them. As well might Hercules have attempted to tidy up the Augean stables with a squirt.

We appealed to the chambermaid. We explained to her that we wanted to wash—to clean ourselves—not to blow bubbles. Could we not have bigger basins and more water and more extensive towels? The chambermaid (a staid old lady of about fifty) did not think that anything better could be done for us by the hotel fraternity of Cologne, and seemed to think that the river was more what we wanted.

I fancied that the old soul was speaking sarcastically, but B. said "No;" she was thinking of the baths alongside the river, and suggested that we should go there. I agreed. It seemed to me that the river—the Rhine—would, if anything could, meet the case. There ought to be plenty of water in it now, after the heavy spring rains.

JEROME K. JEROME

When I saw it, I felt satisfied. I said to B.:

"That's all right, old man; that's the sort of thing we need. That is just the sized river I feel I can get myself clean in this afternoon."

I have heard a good deal in praise of the Rhine, and I am glad to be able to speak well of it myself. I found it most refreshing.

I was, however, sorry that we had washed in it afterwards. I have heard from friends who have travelled since in Germany that we completely spoiled that river for the rest of the season. Not for business purposes, I do not mean. The barge traffic has been, comparatively speaking, uninterfered with. But the tourist trade has suffered terribly. Parties who usually go up the Rhine by steamer have, after looking at the river, gone by train this year. The boat agents have tried to persuade them that the Rhine is always that colour: that it gets like that owing to the dirt and refuse washed down into it during its course among the mountains.

But the tourists have refused to accept this explanation. They have said:

"No. Mountains will account for a good deal, we admit, but not for all *that*. We are acquainted with the ordinary condition of the Rhine, and although muddy, and at times unpleasant, it is passable. As it is this summer, however, we would prefer not to travel upon it. We will wait until after next year's spring-floods."

We went to bed after our wash. To the *blasé* English bed-goer, accustomed all his life to the same old hackneyed style of bed night after night, there is something very pleasantly piquant about the experience of trying to sleep in a German bed. He does not know it is a bed at first. He thinks that someone has been going round the room, collecting all the sacks and cushions and antimacassars and such articles that he has happened to find about, and has piled them up on a wooden tray ready for moving. He rings for the chambermaid, and explains to her that she has shown him into the wrong room. He wanted a bedroom.

She says: "This *is* a bedroom."

He says: "Where's the bed?"

"There!" she says, pointing to the box on which the sacks and antimacassars and cushions lie piled.

"That!" he cries. "How am I going to sleep in that?"

The chambermaid does not know how he is going to sleep there, never having seen a gentleman go to sleep anywhere, and not knowing how they set about it; but suggests that he might try lying down flat, and shutting his eyes.

"But it is not long enough," he says.

The chambermaid thinks he will be able to manage, if he tucks his legs up.

He sees that he will not get anything better, and that he must put up with it.

"Oh, very well!" he says. "Look sharp and get it made, then."

She says: "It is made."

He turns and regards the girl sternly. Is she taking advantage of his being a lonely stranger, far from home and friends, to mock him? He goes over to what she calls the bed, and snatching off the top-most sack from the pile and holding it up, says:

"Perhaps you'll tell me what this is, then?"

"That," says the girl, "that's the bed!"

He is somewhat nonplussed at the unexpected reply.

"Oh!" he says. "Oh! the bed, is it? I thought it was a pincushion! Well, if it is the bed, then what is it doing out here, on the top of everything else? You think that because I'm only a man, I don't understand a bed!"

"That's the proper place for it," responds the chambermaid.

"What! on top?"

"Yes, sir."

"Well, then where are the clothes?"

"Underneath, sir."

"Look here, my good girl," he says; "you don't understand me, or I don't understand you, one or the other. When I go to sleep, I lie on a bed and pull the clothes over me. I don't want to lie on the clothes, and cover myself with the bed. This isn't a comic ballet, you know!"

The girl assures him that there is no mistake about the matter at all. There is the bed, made according to German notions of how a bed should be made. He can make the best of it and try to go to sleep upon it, or he can be sulky and go to sleep on the floor.

He is very much surprised. It looks to him the sort of bed that a man would make for himself on coming home late from a party. But it is no use arguing the matter with the girl.

"All right," he says; "bring me a pillow, and I'll risk it!"

The chambermaid explains that there are two pillows on the bed already, indicating, as she does so, two flat cushions, each one a yard square, placed one on top of the other at one end of the mixture.

"These!" exclaims the weary traveller, beginning to feel that he does not want to go to bed at all. "These are not pillows! I want something to put my head on; not a thing that comes down to the middle of my back! Don't tell me that I've got to sleep on these things!"

But the girl does tell him so, and also implies that she has something else to do than to stand there all day talking bed-gossip with him.

"Well, just show me how to start," he says, "which way you get into it, and then I won't keep you any longer; I'll puzzle out the rest for myself."

She explains the trick to him and leaves, and he undresses and crawls in.

The pillows give him a good deal of worry. He does not know whether he is meant to sit on them or merely to lean up against them. In experimenting upon this point, he bumps his head against the top board of the bedstead. At this, he says, "Oh!" and shoots himself down to the bottom of the bed. Here all his ten toes simultaneously come into sharp contact with the board at the bottom.

Nothing irritates a man more than being rapped over the toes, especially if he feels that he has done nothing to deserve it. He says, "Oh, damn!" this time, and spasmodically doubles up his legs, thus giving his knees a violent blow against the board at the side of the bed. (The German bedstead, be it remembered, is built in the form of a shallow, open box, and the victim is thus completely surrounded by solid pieces of wood with sharp edges. I do not know what species of wood it is that is employed. It is extremely hard, and gives forth a curious musical sound when struck sharply with a bone.)

After this he lies perfectly still for a while, wondering where he is going to be hit next. Finding that nothing happens, he begins to regain confidence, and ventures to gently feel around with his left leg and take stock of his position.

For clothes, he has only a very thin blanket and sheet, and beneath these he feels decidedly chilly. The bed is warm enough, so far as it goes, but there is not enough of it. He draws it up round his chin, and then his feet begin to freeze. He pushes it down over his feet, and then all the top part of him shivers.

He tries to roll up into a ball, so as to get the whole of himself underneath it, but does not succeed; there is always some of him left outside in the cold.

He reflects that a "boneless wonder" or a "man serpent" would be comfortable enough in this bed, and wishes that he had been brought up as a contortionist. If he could only tie his legs round his neck, and tuck his head in under his arm, all would yet be well.

Never having been taught to do any really useful tricks such as these, however, he has to be content to remain spread out, warming a bit of himself at a time.

It is, perhaps, foolish of him, amid so many real troubles, to allow a mere aesthetical consideration to worry him, but as he lies there on his back, looking down at himself, the sight that he presents to himself considerably annoys him. The puffed-up bed, resting on the middle of him, gives him the appearance of a man suffering from some monstrous swelling, or else of some exceptionally well-developed frog that has been turned up the wrong way and does not know how to get on to its legs again.

Another vexation that he has to contend with is, that every time he moves a limb or breathes extra hard, the bed (which is only of down) tumbles off on to the floor.

You cannot lean out of a German bed to pick up anything off the floor, owing to its box-like formation; so he has to scramble out after it, and of course every time he does this he barks both his shins twice against the sides of the bed.

When he has performed this feat for about the tenth time, he concludes that it was madness for him, a mere raw amateur at the business, to think that he could manage a complicated, tricky bed of this sort, that must take even an experienced man all he knows to sleep in it; and gets out and camps on the floor.

At least, that is what I did. B. is accustomed to German beds, and doubled himself up and went off to sleep without the slightest difficulty.

We slept for two hours, and then got up and went back to the railway-station, where we dined. The railway refreshment-room in German towns appears to be as much patronised by the inhabitants of the town as by the travellers passing through. It is regarded as an ordinary restaurant, and used as such by the citizens. We found the dining-room at Cologne station crowded with Cologneists.

All classes of citizens were there, but especially soldiers. There were all sorts of soldiers—soldiers of rank, and soldiers of rank and file; attached soldiers (very much attached, apparently) and soldiers unattached; stout soldiers, thin soldiers; old soldiers, young soldiers. Four very young soldiers sat opposite us, drinking beer. I never saw such young soldiers out by themselves before. They each looked about twelve years old, but may have been thirteen; and they each looked, also, ready and willing to storm a battery, if the order were given to them to do it.

There they sat, raising and lowering their huge mugs of beer, discussing military matters, and rising every now and again to gravely salute some officer as he passed, and to receive as gravely his grave salute in return.

There seemed to be a deal of saluting to be gone through. Officers kept entering and passing through the room in an almost continual stream, and every time one came in sight all the military drinkers and eaters rose and saluted, and remained at the salute until the officer had passed.

One young soldier, who was trying to eat a plate of soup near us, I felt quite sorry for. Every time he got the spoon near his mouth an officer invariably hove in view, and down would have to go the spoon, soup and all, and up he would have to rise. It never seemed to occur to the silly fellow to get under the table and finish his dinner there.

We had half-an-hour to spare between dinner and the starting of our train, and B. suggested that we should go into the cathedral. That is B.'s one weakness, churches. I have the greatest difficulty in getting him past a church-door. We are walking along a street, arm in arm, talking as rationally and even as virtuously as need be, when all at once I find that B. has become silent and abstracted.

I know what it is; he has caught sight of a church. I pretend not to notice any change in him, and endeavour to hurry him on. He lags more and more behind, however, and at last stops altogether.

"Come, come," I say to him, encouragingly, "pull yourself together, and be a man. Don't think about it. Put it behind you, and determine that you *won't* be conquered. Come, we shall be round the corner in another minute, where you won't be able to see it. Take my hand, and let's run!"

He makes a few feeble steps forward with me, and then stops again.

"It's no good, old man," he says, with a sickly smile, so full of pathos that it is impossible to find it in one's heart to feel anything but pity for him. "I can't help it. I have given way to this sort of thing too long. It is too late to reform now. You go on and get a drink somewhere; I'll join you again in a few minutes. Don't worry about me; it's no good."

And back he goes with tottering steps, while I sadly pass on into the nearest cafe, and, over a glass of absinthe or cognac, thank Providence that I learnt to control my craving for churches in early youth, and so am not now like this poor B.

In a little while he comes in, and sits down beside me. There is a wild, unhealthy excitement in his eye, and, under a defiant air of unnatural gaiety, he attempts to hide his consciousness of guilt.

"It was a lovely altar-cloth," he whispers to me, with an enthusiasm that only makes one sorrow for him the more, so utterly impossible does it cause all hope of cure to seem. "And they've got a coffin in the north crypt that is simply a poem. I never enjoyed a sarcophagus more in all my life."

I do not say much at the time; it would be useless. But after the day is done, and we are standing beside our little beds, and all around is as silent as one can expect it to be in an hotel where people seem to be arriving all night long with heavy luggage, and to be all, more or less, in trouble, I argue with him, and gently reprove him. To avoid the appearance of sermonising as much as possible, I put it on mere grounds of expediency.

"How are we to find time," I say, "to go to all the places that we really ought to go to—to all the cafes and theatres and music-halls and beer-gardens and dancing-saloons that we want to visit—if you waste half the precious day loafing about churches and cathedrals?"

He is deeply moved, and promises to swear off. He vows, with tears in his voice, that he will never enter a church-door again. But next morning, when the temptation comes, all his good resolutions are swept away, and again he yields. It is no good being angry with him, because he evidently does really try; but there is something about the mere odour of a church that he simply cannot withstand.

Not knowing, then, that this weakness of his for churches was so strong, I made no objection to the proposed visit to Cologne Cathedral, and, accordingly, towards it we wended our way. B. has seen it before, and knows all about it. He tells me it was begun about the middle of the thirteenth century, and was only completed ten years ago. It seems to me that there must have been gross delay on the part of the builder. Why, a plumber would be ashamed to take as long as that over a job!

B. also asserts that the two towers are the highest church towers in the world. I dispute this, and deprecate the towers generally. B. warmly defends them. He says they are higher than any building in Europe, except the Eiffel Tower.

"Oh, dear no!" I say, "there are many buildings higher than they in Europe—to say nothing of Asia and America."

I have no authority for making this assertion. As a matter of fact, I know nothing whatever about the matter. I merely say it to irritate B. He appears to take a sort of personal interest in the building, and enlarges upon its beauties and advantages with as much fervour as if he were an auctioneer trying to sell the place.

He retorts that the towers are 512 feet high.

I say:

"Nonsense! Somebody has imposed upon you, because they see you are a foreigner."

He becomes quite angry at this, and says he can show me the figures in the guide-book.

"The guide-book!" I reply, scornfully. "You'll believe a newspaper next!"

B. asks me, indignantly, what height I should say they are, then. I examine them critically for a few minutes, and then give it as my opinion that they do not exceed 510 feet at the very outside. B. seems annoyed with me, and we enter the church in silence.

There is little to be said about a cathedral. Except to the professional sightseer, one is very much like another. Their beauty to me lies, not in the paintings and sculpture they give houseroom to, nor in the bones and bric-a-brac piled up in their cellars, but in themselves—their echoing vastness, their deep silence.

Above the little homes of men, above the noisy teeming streets, they rise like some soft strain of perfect music, cleaving its way amid the jangle of discordant notes. Here, where the voices of the world sound faint; here, where the city's glamour comes not in, it is good to rest for a while—if only the pestering guides would leave one alone—and think.

There is much help in Silence. From its touch we gain renewed life. Silence is to the Soul what his Mother Earth was to Briareus. From contact with it we rise healed of our hurts and strengthened for the fight.

Amid the babel of the schools we stand bewildered and affrighted. Silence gives us peace and hope. Silence teaches us no creed, only that God's arms are around the universe.

How small and unimportant seem all our fretful troubles and ambitions when we stand with them in our hand before the great calm face of Silence! We smile at them ourselves, and are ashamed.

Silence teaches us how little we are—how great we are. In the world's market-places we are tinkers, tailors, apothecaries, thieves—respectable or otherwise, as the case may be—mere atoms of a mighty machine—mere insects in a vast hive.

It is only in Silence that it comes home to us that we are something much greater than this—that we are *men*, with all the universe and all eternity before us.

It is in Silence we hear the voice of Truth. The temples and the marts of men echo all night and day to the clamour of lies and shams and quackeries. But in Silence falsehood cannot live. You cannot float a lie on Silence. A lie has to be puffed aloft, and kept from falling by men's breath. Leave a lie on the bosom of Silence, and it sinks. A truth floats there fair and stately, like some stout ship upon a deep ocean. Silence buoys her up lovingly for all men to see. Not until she has grown worn-out and rotten, and is no longer a truth, will the waters of Silence close over her.

Silence is the only real thing we can lay hold of in this world of passing dreams. Time is a shadow that will vanish with the twilight of humanity; but Silence is a part of the eternal. All things that are true and lasting have been taught to men's hearts by Silence.

Among all nations, there should be vast temples raised where the people might worship Silence and listen to it, for it is the voice of God.

These fair churches and cathedrals that men have reared around them throughout the world, have been built as homes for mere creeds—this one for Protestantism, that one for Romanism, another for Mahomedanism. But God's Silence dwells in all alike, only driven forth at times by the tinkling of bells and the mumbling of prayers; and, in them, it is good to sit awhile and have communion with her.

We strolled round, before we came out. Just by the entrance to the choir an official stopped me, and asked me if I wanted to go and see a lot of fal-lal things he had got on show—relics and bones, and old masters, and such-like Wardour-street rubbish.

I told him, "No"; and attempted to pass on, but he said:

"No, no! You don't pay, you don't go in there," and shut the gate.

He said this sentence in English; and the precision and fluency with which he delivered it rather suggested the idea that it was a phrase much in request, and one that he had had a good deal of practice in.

It is very prevalent throughout Germany, this custom of not allowing you to go in to see a thing unless you pay.

The Rhine!—How History is Written.—Complicated Villages.—How a Peaceful Community Was Very Much Upset.—The German Railway Guard.—His Passion for Tickets.—We Diffuse Comfort and Joy Wherever We Go, Gladdening the Weary, and Bringing Smiles to Them that Weep.—"Tickets, Please."—Hunting Experiences.—A Natural Mistake.—Free Acrobatic Performance by the Guard.—The Railway Authorities' Little Joke.—Why We Should Think of the Sorrows of Others.

We returned to the station just in time to secure comfortable seats, and at 5.10 steamed out upon our fifteen hours' run to Munich. From Bonn to Mayence the line keeps by the side of the Rhine nearly the whole of the way, and we had a splendid view of the river, with the old-world towns and villages that cluster round its bank, the misty mountains that make early twilight upon its swiftly rolling waves, the castled crags and precipices that rise up sheer and majestic from its margin, the wooded rocks that hang with threatening frown above its sombre depths, the ruined towers and turrets that cap each point along its shores, the pleasant isles that stud like gems its broad expanse of waters.

Few things in this world come up to expectation, especially those things of which one has been led to expect much, and about which one has heard a good deal. With this philosophy running in my head, I was prepared to find the Rhine a much over-rated river.

I was pleasantly disappointed. The panorama which unfolded itself before our eyes, as we sped along through the quiet twilight that was deepening into starry night, was wonderfully beautiful, entrancing and expressive.

I do not intend to describe it to you. To do justice to the theme, I should have to be even a more brilliant and powerful writer than I am. To attempt the subject, without doing it justice, would be a waste of your time, sweet reader, and of mine—a still more important matter.

I confess it was not my original intention to let you off so easily. I started with the idea of giving you a rapid but glowing and eloquent word-picture of the valley of the Rhine from Cologne to Mayence. For background, I thought I would sketch in the historical and legendary events connected with the district, and against this, for a foreground, I would draw, in vivid colours, the modern aspect of the scene, with remarks and observations thereon.

Here are my rough notes, made for the purpose:—

Mems. for Chapter on Rhine: "Constantine the Great used to come here—so did Agrippa. Caesar had a good deal to do with the Rhine—also Nero's mother."

(To the reader.—The brevity of these memoranda renders their import, at times, confusing. For instance, this means that Caesar and Nero's mother both had a good deal to do with the Rhine; not that Caesar had a good deal to do with Nero's mother. I explain this because I should be sorry to convey any false impression concerning either the lady or Caesar. Scandal is a thing abhorrent to my nature.)

Notes continued: "The Ubii did something on the right bank of the Rhine at an early period, and afterwards were found on the other side. (Expect the Ubii were a tribe; but make sure of this, as they might be something in the fossil line.) Cologne was the cradle of German art. Talk about art and the old masters. Treat them in a kindly and gentle spirit. They are dead now. Saint Ursula was murdered at Cologne, with eleven thousand virgin attendants. There must have been quite a party of them. Draw powerful and pathetic imaginary picture of the slaughter. Say something about the Emperor Maximilian. Call him 'the mighty Maximilian.' Mention Charlemagne (a good deal should be made out of Charlemagne) and the Franks. (Find out all about the Franks, and where they lived, and what has become of them.) Sketch the various contests between the Romans and the Goths. (Read up 'Gibbon' for this, unless you can get enough out of *Mangnall's Questions*.) Give picturesque account—with comments—of the battles between the citizens of Cologne and their haughty archbishops. Bring in the Minne-singers, especially Walter von Vogelweid; make him sing under a castle-wall somewhere, and let the girl die. Talk about Albert Durer. Criticise his style. Say it's flat. (If possible, find out if it *is* flat.) "The rat tower on the Rhine," near Bingen. Describe the place and tell the whole story. Don't spin it out too long, because everybody knows it. "The Brothers of Bornhofen," story connected with the twin castles of Sterrenberg and Liebenstein, Conrad and Heinrich—brothers—both love Hildegarde. She was very beautiful. Heinrich generously refuses to marry the beautiful Hildegarde, and goes away to the Crusades, leaving her to his brother Conrad. Conrad considers over the matter for a year or two, and then *he* decides that he won't marry her either, but will leave her for his brother Heinrich, and *he* goes off to the Crusades, from whence he returns, a few years later on, with a Grecian bride. The beautiful H., muddled up between the pair of them, and the victim of too much generosity, gets sulky (don't blame her), and shuts herself up in a lonely part of the castle, and won't see anybody for years. Chivalrous Heinrich returns, and is wild that his brother C. has not married the beautiful H. It does not occur to him to marry the girl even then. The feverish yearning displayed by each of these two brothers, that the other one should marry the beloved Hildegarde, is very touching. Heinrich draws his sword, and throws himself upon his brother C. to kill him. The beautiful Hildegarde, however, throws herself between them and reconciliates them, and then, convinced that neither of them means business, and naturally disgusted with the whole affair, retires into a nunnery. Conrad's Grecian bride subsequently throws herself away on another man, upon which Conrad throws himself on his brother H.'s breast, and they swear eternal friendship. (Make it pathetic. Pretend you have sat amid the ruins in the moonlight, and give the scene—with ghosts.) "Rolandseck," near Bonn. Tell the story of Roland and Hildegunde (see *Baedeker*, p. 66). Don't make it too long, because it is so much like the other. Describe the funeral? The "Watch Tower on the Rhine" below Audernach. Query, isn't there a song about this? If so, put it in. Coblentz and Ehrenbreitstein. Great fortresses. Call them "the Frowning Sentinels of the State." Make reflections on the German army, also on war generally. Chat about Frederick the Great. (Read Carlyle's history of him, and pick out the interesting bits.) The Drachenfels. Quote Byron. Moralise about ruined castles generally, and describe the middle ages, with your views and opinions on same."

There is much more of it, but that is sufficient to let you see the scheme I had in my head. I have not carried out my scheme, because, when I came to reflect upon the matter, it seemed to me that the idea would develop into something that would be more in the nature of a history of Europe than a chapter in a tourist's diary, and I determined not to waste my time upon it, until there arose a greater public demand for a new History of Europe than there appears to exist at present.

"Besides," I argued to myself, "such a work would be just the very thing with which to beguile the tedium of a long imprisonment. At some future time I may be glad of a labour of this magnitude to occupy a period of involuntary inaction."

"This is the sort of thing," I said to myself, "to save up for Holloway or Pentonville."

It would have been a very enjoyable ride altogether, that evening's spin along the banks of the Rhine, if I had not been haunted at the time by the idea that I should have to write an account of it next day in my diary. As it was, I enjoyed it as a man enjoys a dinner when he has got to make a speech after it, or as a critic enjoys a play.

We passed such odd little villages every here and there. Little places so crowded up between the railway and the river that there was no room in them for any streets. All the houses were jumbled up together just anyhow, and how any man who lived in the middle could get home without climbing over half the other houses in the place I could not make out. They were the sort of villages where a man's mother-in-law, coming to pay him a visit, might wander around all day, hearing him, and even now and then seeing him, yet never being able to get at him in consequence of not knowing the way in.

A drunken man, living in one of these villages, could never hope to get home. He would have to sit down outside, and wait till his head was clear.

We witnessed the opening scenes of a very amusing little comedy at one of the towns where the train drew up. The chief characters were played by an active young goat, a small boy, an elderly man and a woman, parents of the small boy and owners of the goat, and a dog.

First we heard a yell, and then, from out a cottage opposite the station, bounded an innocent and happy goat, and gambolled around. A long rope, one end of which was fastened to his neck, trailed behind him. After the goat (in the double sense of the phrase) came a child. The child tried to catch the goat by means of the rope, caught itself in the rope instead, and went down with a bump and a screech. Whereupon a stout woman, the boy's mother apparently, ran out from the cottage, and also made for the goat. The goat flew down the road, and the woman flew after it. At the first corner, the woman trod on the rope, and then *she* went down with a bump and a screech. Then the goat turned and ran up the street, and, as it passed the cottage, the father ran out and tried to stop it. He was an old man, but still seemed to have plenty of vigour in him. He evidently guessed how his wife and child had gone down, and he endeavoured to avoid the rope and to skip over it when it came near him. But the goat's movements were too erratic for him. His turn came, and he trod on the rope, and went down in the middle of the road, opposite his own door, with a thud that shook us all up against each other as we stood looking out of the carriage-window, and sat there and cursed the goat. Then out ran a dog, barking furiously, and he went for the goat, and got the end of the rope in his teeth and held on to it like grim death. Away went the goat, at his end of the rope, and, with him, the dog at the other end. Between them, they kept the rope about six inches above the ground, and with it they remorselessly mowed down every living thing they came across in that once peaceful village. In the course of less than half a minute we counted fourteen persons sitting down in the middle of the road. Eight of them were cursing the goat, four were cursing the dog, and two of them were cursing the old man for keeping the goat, one of these two, and the more violent one, being the man's own wife.

The train left at this juncture. We entreated the railway officials to let us stop and see the show out. The play was becoming quite interesting. It was so full of movement. But they said that we were half-an-hour late as it was, and that they dared not.

We leaned out of the window, and watched for as long as we could; and after the village was lost to view in the distance, we could still, by listening carefully, hear the thuds, as one after another of the inhabitants sat down and began to swear.

At about eleven o'clock we had some beer—you can generally obtain such light refreshment as bottled beer and coffee and rolls from the guard on a through long-distance train in Germany—took off our boots, and saying "Good-night" to each other, made a great show of going to sleep. But we never succeeded in getting there. They wanted to see one's ticket too often for one to get fairly off.

Every few minutes, so it seemed to me, though in reality the intervals may perhaps have been longer, a ghostly face would appear at the carriage-window, and ask to see our tickets.

Whenever a German railway-guard feels lonesome, and does not know what else to do with himself, he takes a walk round the train, and gets the passengers to show him their tickets, after which he returns to his box cheered and refreshed. Some people rave about sunsets and mountains and old masters; but to the German railway-guard the world can show nothing more satisfying, more inspiring, than the sight of a railway-ticket.

Nearly all the German railway officials have this same craving for tickets. If only they get somebody to show them a railway-ticket, they are happy. It seemed a harmless weakness of theirs, and B. and I decided that it would be only kind to humour them in it during our stay.

Accordingly, whenever we saw a German railway official standing about, looking sad and weary, we went up to him and showed him our tickets. The sight was like a ray of sunshine to him; and all his care was immediately forgotten. If we had not a ticket with us at the time, we went and bought one. A mere single third to the next station would gladden him sufficiently in most cases; but if the poor fellow appeared very woe-begone, and as if he wanted more than ordinary cheering up, we got him a second-class return.

For the purpose of our journey to Ober-Ammergau and back, we each carried with us a folio containing some ten or twelve first-class tickets between different towns, covering in all a distance of some thousand miles; and one afternoon, at Munich, seeing a railway official, a cloak-room keeper, who they told us had lately lost his aunt, and who looked exceptionally dejected, I proposed to B. that we should take this man into a quiet corner, and both of us show him all our tickets at once—the whole twenty or twenty-four of them—and let him take them in his hand and look at them for as long as he liked. I wanted to comfort him.

B., however, advised against the suggestion. He said that even if it did not turn the man's head (and it was more than probable that it would), so much jealousy would be created against him among the other railway people throughout Germany, that his life would be made a misery to him.

So we bought and showed him a first-class return to the next station but one; and it was quite pathetic to watch the poor fellow's face brighten up at the sight, and to see the faint smile creep back to the lips from which it had so long been absent.

But at times, one wishes that the German railway official would control his passion for tickets—or, at least, keep it within due bounds.

Even the most kindly-hearted man grows tired of showing his ticket all day and night long, and the middle of a wearisome journey is not the proper time for a man to come to the carriage-window and clamour to see your "billet."

JEROME K. JEROME

You are weary and sleepy. You do not know where your ticket is. You are not quite sure that you have got a ticket; or if you ever had one, somebody has taken it away from you. You have put it by very carefully, thinking that it would not be wanted for hours, and have forgotten where.

There are eleven pockets in the suit you have on, and five more in the overcoat on the rack. Maybe, it is in one of those pockets. If not, it is possibly in one of the bags—somewhere, or in your pocket-book, if you only knew where that was, or your purse.

You begin a search. You stand up and shake yourself. Then you have another feel all over. You look round in the course of the proceedings; and the sight of the crowd of curious faces watching you, and of the man in uniform waiting with his eye fixed severely upon you, convey to you, in your then state of confusion, the momentary idea that this is a police-court scene, and that if the ticket is found upon you, you will probably get five years.

Upon this you vehemently protest your innocence.

"I tell you I haven't got it!" you exclaim;—"never seen the gentleman's ticket. You let me go! I—"

Here the surprise of your fellow-passengers recalls you to yourself, and you proceed on your exploration. You overhaul the bags, turning everything out on to the floor, muttering curses on the whole railway system of Germany as you do so. Then you feel in your boots. You make everybody near you stand up to see if they are sitting upon it, and you go down on your knees and grovel for it under the seat.

"You didn't throw it out of the window with your sandwiches, did you?" asks your friend.

"No! Do you think I'm a fool?" you answer, irritably. "What should I want to do that for?"

On going systematically over yourself for about the twentieth time, you discover it in your waistcoat pocket, and for the next half-hour you sit and wonder how you came to miss it on the previous nineteen occasions.

Meanwhile, during this trying scene, the conduct of the guard has certainly not tended to allay your anxiety and nervousness. All the time that you have been looking for your ticket, he has been doing silly tricks on the step outside, imperilling his life by every means that experience and ingenuity can suggest.

The train is going at the rate of thirty miles an hour, the express speed in Germany, and a bridge comes in sight crossing over the line.

On seeing this bridge, the guard, holding on by the window, leans his body as far back as ever it will go. You look at him, and then at the rapidly-nearing bridge, and calculate that the arch will just take his head off without injuring any other part of him whatever, and you wonder whether the head will be jerked into the carriage or will fall outside.

When he is three inches off the bridge, he pulls himself up straight, and the brickwork, as the train dashes through, kills a fly that was trespassing on the upper part of his right ear.

Then, when the bridge is passed, and the train is skirting the very edge of a precipice, so that a stone dropped just outside the window would tumble straight down 300 feet, he suddenly lets go, and, balancing himself on the foot-board without holding on to anything, commences to dance a sort of Teutonic cellar-flap, and to warm his body by flinging his arms about in the manner of cabmen on a cold day.

The first essential to comfortable railway travelling in Germany is to make up your mind not to care a rap whether the guard gets killed in the course of the journey or not. Any tender feeling towards the guard makes railway travelling in the Fatherland a simple torture.

At five A.M. (how fair and sweet and fresh the earth looks in the early morning! Those lazy people who lie in bed till eight or nine miss half the beauty of the day, if they but knew it. It is only we who rise early that really enjoy Nature properly) I gave up trying to get to sleep, and made my way to the dressing-room at the end of the car, and had a wash.

It is difficult to wash in these little places, because the cars shake so; and when you have got both your hands and half your head in the basin, and are unable to protect yourself, the sides of the room, and the water-tap and the soap-dish, and other cowardly things, take a mean advantage of your helplessness to punch you as hard as ever they can; and when you back away from these, the door swings open and slaps you from behind.

I succeeded, however, in getting myself fairly wet all over, even if I did nothing else, and then I looked about for a towel. Of course, there was no towel. That is the trick. The idea of the railway authorities is to lure the passenger, by providing him with soap and water and a basin, into getting himself thoroughly soaked, and then to let it dawn upon him that there is no towel. That is their notion of fun!

I thought of the handkerchiefs in my bag, but to get to them I

JEROME K. JEROME

should have to pass compartments containing ladies, and I was only in early morning dress.

So I had to wipe myself with a newspaper which I happened to have in my pocket, and a more unsatisfactory thing to dry oneself upon I cannot conceive.

I woke up B. when I got back to the carriage, and persuaded him to go and have a wash; and in listening to the distant sound of his remarks when he likewise discovered that there was no towel, the recollection of my own discomfiture passed gently away.

Ah! how true it is, as good people tell us, that in thinking of the sorrows of others, we learn to forget our own!

For fifty miles before one reaches Munich, the land is flat, stale, and apparently very unprofitable, and there is little to interest the looker-out. He sits straining his eyes towards the horizon, eagerly longing for some sign of the city to come in sight.

It lies very low, however, and does all it can to escape observation; and it is not until he is almost within its streets that he discovers it.

The Rest of Sunday, the 25th

A t Munich we left our luggage at the station, and went in search of
breakfast. Of course, at eight o'clock in the morning none of the
big cafes were open; but at length, beside some gardens, we found an
old-fashioned looking restaurant, from which came a pleasant odour
of coffee and hot onions; and walking through and seating ourselves at
one of the little tables, placed out under the trees, we took the bill of
fare in our hands, and summoned the waiter to our side.

I ordered the breakfast. I thought it would be a good opportunity for
me to try my German. I ordered coffee and rolls as a groundwork. I got
over that part of my task very easily. With the practice I had had during the
last two days, I could have ordered coffee and rolls for forty. Then I foraged
round for luxuries, and ordered a green salad. I had some difficulty at first
in convincing the man that it was not a boiled cabbage that I wanted, but
succeeded eventually in getting that silly notion out of his head.

I still had a little German left, even after that. So I ordered an
omelette also.

"Tell him a savoury one," said B., "or he will be bringing us something
full of hot jam and chocolate-creams. You know their style."

"Oh, yes," I answered. "Of course. Yes. Let me see. What is the
German for savoury?"

"Savoury?" mused B. "Oh! ah! hum! Bothered if I know! Confound
the thing—I can't think of it!"

I could not think of it either. As a matter of fact, I never knew it. We
tried the man with French. We said:

"*Une omelette aux fines herbes.*"

As he did not appear to understand that, we gave it him in bad
English. We twisted and turned the unfortunate word "savoury" into
sounds so quaint, so sad, so unearthly, that you would have thought

they might have touched the heart of a savage. This stoical Teuton, however, remained unmoved. Then we tried pantomime.

Pantomime is to language what marmalade, according to the label on the pot, is to butter, "an excellent (occasional) substitute." But its powers as an interpreter of thought are limited. At least, in real life they are so. As regards a ballet, it is difficult to say what is not explainable by pantomime. I have seen the bad man in a ballet convey to the *premiere danseuse* by a subtle movement of the left leg, together with some slight assistance from the drum, the heartrending intelligence that the lady she had been brought up to believe was her mother was in reality only her aunt by marriage. But then it must be borne in mind that the *premiere danseuse* is a lady whose quickness of perception is altogether unique. The *premiere danseuse* knows precisely what a gentleman means when he twirls round forty-seven times on one leg, and then stands on his head. The average foreigner would, in all probability, completely misunderstand the man.

A friend of mine once, during a tour in the Pyrenees, tried to express gratitude by means of pantomime. He arrived late one evening at a little mountain inn, where the people made him very welcome, and set before him their best; and he, being hungry, appreciated their kindness, and ate a most excellent supper.

Indeed, so excellent a meal did he make, and so kind and attentive were his hosts to him, that, after supper, he felt he wanted to thank them, and to convey to them some idea of how pleased and satisfied he was.

He could not explain himself in language. He only knew enough Spanish to just ask for what he wanted—and even to do that he had to be careful not to want much. He had not got as far as sentiment and emotion at that time. Accordingly he started to express himself in action. He stood up and pointed to the empty table where the supper had been, then opened his mouth and pointed down his throat. Then he patted that region of his anatomy where, so scientific people tell us, supper goes to, and smiled.

He has a rather curious smile, has my friend. He himself is under the impression that there is something very winning in it, though, also, as he admits, a touch of sadness. They use it in his family for keeping the children in order.

The people of the inn seemed rather astonished at his behaviour. They regarded him, with troubled looks, and then gathered together among themselves and consulted in whispers.

"I evidently have not made myself sufficiently clear to these simple peasants," said my friend to himself. "I must put more vigour into this show."

Accordingly he rubbed and patted that part of himself to which I have previously alluded—and which, being a modest and properly brought-up young man, nothing on earth shall induce me to mention more explicitly—with greater energy than ever, and added another inch or two of smile; and he also made various graceful movements indicative, as he thought, of friendly feeling and contentment.

At length a ray of intelligence burst upon the faces of his hosts, and they rushed to a cupboard and brought out a small black bottle.

"Ah! that's done it," thought my friend. "Now they have grasped my meaning. And they are pleased that I am pleased, and are going to insist on my drinking a final friendly bumper of wine with them, the good old souls!"

They brought the bottle over, and poured out a wineglassful, and handed it to him, making signs that he should drink it off quickly.

"Ah!" said my friend to himself, as he took the glass and raised it to the light, and winked at it wickedly, "this is some rare old spirit peculiar to the district—some old heirloom kept specially for the favoured guest."

And he held the glass aloft and made a speech, in which he wished long life and many grand-children to the old couple, and a handsome husband to the daughter, and prosperity to the whole village. They could not understand him, he knew; but he thought there might be that in his tones and gestures from which they would gather the sense of what he was saying, and understand how kindly he felt towards them all. When he had finished, he put his hand upon his heart and smiled some more, and then tossed the liquor off at a gulp.

Three seconds later he discovered that it was a stringent and trustworthy emetic that he had swallowed. His audience had mistaken his signs of gratitude for efforts on his part to explain to them that he was poisoned, or, at all events, was suffering from acute and agonising indigestion, and had done what they could to comfort him.

The drug that they had given him was not one of those common, cheap medicines that lose their effect before they have been in the system half-an-hour. He felt that it would be useless to begin another supper then, even if he could get one, and so he went to bed a good deal hungrier and a good deal less refreshed than when he arrived at the inn.

JEROME K. JEROME

Gratitude is undoubtedly a thing that should not be attempted by the amateur pantomimist.

"Savoury" is another. B. and I very nearly did ourselves a serious internal injury, trying to express it. We slaved like cab-horses at it—for about five minutes, and succeeded in conveying to the mind of the waiter that we wanted to have a game at dominoes.

Then, like a beam of sunlight to a man lost in some dark, winding cave, came to me the reflection that I had in my pocket a German conversation book.

How stupid of me not to have thought of it before. Here had we been racking our brains and our bodies, trying to explain our wants to an uneducated German, while, all the time, there lay to our hands a book specially written and prepared to assist people out of the very difficulty into which we had fallen—a book carefully compiled with the express object of enabling English travellers who, like ourselves, only spoke German in a dilettante fashion, to make their modest requirements known throughout the Fatherland, and to get out of the country alive and uninjured.

I hastily snatched the book from my pocket, and commenced to search for dialogues dealing with the great food question. There were none!

There were lengthy and passionate "Conversations with a laundress" about articles that I blush to remember. Some twenty pages of the volume were devoted to silly dialogues between an extraordinarily patient shoemaker and one of the most irritating and constitutionally dissatisfied customers that an unfortunate shop-keeper could possibly be cursed with; a customer who, after twaddling for about forty minutes, and trying on, apparently, every pair of boots in the place, calmly walks out with:

"Ah! well, I shall not purchase anything to-day. Good-morning!"

The shopkeeper's reply, by-the-by, is not given. It probably took the form of a boot-jack, accompanied by phrases deemed useless for the purposes of the Christian tourist.

There was really something remarkable about the exhaustiveness of this "conversation at the shoemaker's." I should think the book must have been written by someone who suffered from corns. I could have gone to a German shoemaker with this book and have talked the man's head off.

Then there were two pages of watery chatter "on meeting a friend in the street"—"Good-morning, sir (or madam)." "I wish you a merry

Christmas." "How is your mother?" As if a man who hardly knew enough German to keep body and soul together, would want to go about asking after the health of a foreign person's mother.

There were also "conversations in the railway carriage," conversations between travelling lunatics, apparently, and dialogues "during the passage." "How do you feel now?" "Pretty well as yet; but I cannot say how long it will last." "Oh, what waves! I now feel very unwell and shall go below. Ask for a basin for me." Imagine a person who felt like that wanting to know the German for it.

At the end of the book were German proverbs and "Idiomatic Phrases," by which latter would appear to be meant in all languages, "phrases for the use of idiots":—"A sparrow in the hand is better than a pigeon on the roof."—"Time brings roses."—"The eagle does not catch flies."—"One should not buy a cat in a sack,"—as if there were a large class of consumers who habitually did purchase their cats in that way, thus enabling unscrupulous dealers to palm off upon them an inferior cat, and whom it was accordingly necessary to advise against the custom.

I skimmed through all this nonsense, but not a word could I discover anywhere about a savoury omelette. Under the head of "Eating and Drinking," I found a short vocabulary; but it was mainly concerned with "raspberries" and "figs" and "medlars" (whatever they may be; I never heard of them myself), and "chestnuts," and such like things that a man hardly ever wants, even when he is in his own country. There was plenty of oil and vinegar, and pepper and salt and mustard in the list, but nothing to put them on. I could have had a hard-boiled egg, or a slice of ham; but I did not want a hard-boiled egg, or a slice of ham. I wanted a savoury omelette; and that was an article of diet that the authors of this "Handy Little Guide," as they termed it in their preface, had evidently never heard of.

Since my return home, I have, out of curiosity, obtained three or four "English-German Dialogues" and "Conversation Books," intended to assist the English traveller in his efforts to make himself understood by the German people, and I have come to the conclusion that the work I took out with me was the most sensible and practical of the lot.

Finding it utterly hopeless to explain ourselves to the waiter, we let the thing go, and trusted to Providence; and in about ten minutes the man brought us a steaming omelette, with about a pound of strawberry jam inside, and powdered sugar all over the outside. We put a deal of pepper and salt on it to try and counteract the flavour of the sweets, but we did not really enjoy it even then.

After breakfast we got a time-table, and looked out for a train to Ober-Ammergau. I found one which started at 3.10. It seemed a very nice train indeed; it did not stop anywhere. The railway authorities themselves were evidently very proud of it, and had printed particulars of it in extra thick type. We decided to patronise it.

To pass away the time, we strolled about the city. Munich is a fine, handsome, open town, full of noble streets and splendid buildings; but in spite of this and of its hundred and seventy thousand inhabitants, an atmosphere of quiet and provincialism hovers over it. There is but little traffic on ordinary occasions along its broad ways, and customers in its well-stocked shops are few and far between. This day being Sunday, it was busier than usual, and its promenades were thronged with citizens and country folk in holiday attire, among whom the Southern peasants, wearing their quaint, centuries-old costume, stood out in picturesque relief. Fashion, in its world-wide crusade against variety and its bitter contest with form and colour, has recoiled, defeated for the present from the mountain fastnesses of Bavaria. Still, as Sunday or gala-day comes round, the broad-shouldered, sunburnt shepherd of the Oberland dons his gay green-embroidered jacket over his snowy shirt, fastens his short knee-breeches with a girdle round his waist, claps his high, feather-crowned hat upon his waving curls, and with bare legs, shod in mighty boots, strides over the hill-sides to his Gretchen's door.

She is waiting for him, you may be sure, ready dressed; and a very sweet, old-world picture she makes, standing beneath the great overhanging gables of the wooden chalet. She, too, favours the national green; but, as relief, there is no lack of bonny red ribbons, to flutter in the wind, and, underneath the ornamented skirt, peeps out a bright-hued petticoat. Around her ample breast she wears a dark tight-fitting bodice, laced down the front. (I think this garment is called a stomacher, but I am not sure, as I have never liked to ask.) Her square shoulders are covered with the whitest of white linen. Her sleeves are also white; and being very full, and of some soft lawnlike material, suggest the idea of folded wings. Upon her flaxen hair is perched a saucy round green hat. The buckles of her dainty shoes, the big eyes in her pretty face, are all four very bright. One feels one would like much to change places for the day with Hans.

Arm-in-arm, looking like some china, but exceedingly substantial china, shepherd and shepherdess, they descend upon the town. One rubs one's eyes and stares after them as they pass. They seem to have stepped from the pictured pages of one of those old story-books that we learnt to love, sitting beside the high brass guard that kept ourselves and the nursery-fire from doing each other any serious injury, in the days when the world was much bigger than it is now, and much more real and interesting.

Munich and the country round about it make a great exchange of peoples every Sunday. In the morning, trainload after trainload of villagers and mountaineers pour into the town, and trainload after trainload of good and other citizens steam out to spend the day in wood and valley, and upon lake and mountain-side.

We went into one or two of the beer-halls—not into the swell cafes, crowded with tourists and Munich masherdom, but into the low-ceilinged, smoke-grimed cellars where the life of the people is to be seen.

The ungenteel people in a country are so much more interesting than the gentlefolks. One lady or gentleman is painfully like every other lady or gentleman. There is so little individuality, so little character, among the upper circles of the world. They talk like each other, they think and act like each other, they dress like each other, and look very much like each other. We gentlefolks only play at living. We have our rules and regulations for the game, which must not be infringed. Our unwritten guide-books direct us what to do and what to say at each turn of the meaningless sport.

To those at the bottom of the social pyramid, however, who stand with their feet upon the earth, Nature is not a curious phenomenon to be looked down at and studied, but a living force to be obeyed. They front grim, naked Life, face to face, and wrestle with it through the darkness; and, as did the angel that strove with Jacob, it leaves its stamp upon them.

There is only one type of a gentleman. There are five hundred types of men and women. That is why I always seek out and frequent the places where the common people congregate, in preference to the haunts of respectability. I have to be continually explaining all this to my friends, to account to them for what they call my love of low life.

With a mug of beer before me, and a pipe in my mouth, I could sit for hours contentedly, and watch the life that ebbs and flows into and out of these old ale-kitchens.

The brawny peasant lads bring in their lasses to treat them to the beloved nectar of Munich, together with a huge onion. How they enjoy themselves! What splendid jokes they have! How they laugh and roar and sing! At one table sit four old fellows, playing cards. How full of character is each gnarled face. One is eager, quick, vehement. How his eyes dance! You can read his every thought upon his face. You know when he is going to dash down the king with a shout of triumph on the queen. His neighbour looks calm, slow, and dogged, but wears a confident expression. The game proceeds, and you watch and wait for him to play the winning cards that you feel sure he holds. He must intend to win. Victory is written in his face. No! he loses. A seven was the highest card in his hand. Everyone turns to him, surprised. He laughs—A difficult man to deal with, that, in other matters besides cards. A man whose thoughts lie a good deal below his skin.

Opposite, a cross-looking old woman clamours for sausages, gets them, and seems crosser than ever. She scowls round on everyone, with a malignant expression that is quite terrifying. A small dog comes and sits down in front of her, and grins at her. Still, with the same savage expression of hatred towards all living things, she feeds him with sausage at the end of a fork, regarding him all the while with an aspect of such concentrated dislike, that one wonders it does not interfere with his digestion. In a corner, a stout old woman talks incessantly to a solemn-looking man, who sits silent and drinks steadily. It is evident that he can stand her conversation just so long as he has a mug of beer in front of him. He has brought her in here to give her a treat. He will let her have her talk out while he drinks. Heavens! how she does talk! She talks without movement, without expression; her voice never varies, it flows on, and on, and on, like a great resistless river. Four young artisans come clamping along in their hob-nailed boots, and seating themselves at one of the rude wooden tables, call for beer. With their arms round the waist of the utterly indifferent Fraulein, they shout and laugh and sing. Nearly all the young folks here are laughing—looking forward to life. All the old folks are talking, remembering it.

What grand pictures some of these old, seared faces round us would make, if a man could only paint them—paint all that is in them, all the tragedy—and comedy that the great playwright, Life, has written upon the withered skins! Joys and sorrows, sordid hopes and fears, child-like strivings to be good, mean selfishness and grand unselfishness, have helped to fashion these old wrinkled faces. The curves of cunning and kindliness lurk round these fading eyes. The lines of greed hover about these bloodless lips, that have so often been tight-pressed in patient heroism.

We Dine.—A Curious Dish.—"A Feeling of Sadness Comes
O'er Me."—The German Cigar.—The Handsomest Match
in Europe.—"How Easy 'tis for Friends to Drift Apart,"
especially in a place like Munich Railway Station.—The
Victim of Fate.—A Faithful Bradshaw.—Among the
Mountains.—Prince and Pauper.—A Modern Romance.—
Arrival at Oberau.—Wise and Foolish Pilgrims.—An
Interesting Drive.—Ettal and its Monastery.—We Reach
the Goal of our Pilgrimage.

At one o'clock we turned into a restaurant for dinner. The Germans
themselves always dine in the middle of the day, and a very
substantial meal they make of it. At the hotels frequented by tourists
table d'hote is, during the season, fixed for about six or seven, but this is
only done to meet the views of foreign customers.

I mention that we had dinner, not because I think that the
information will prove exciting to the reader, but because I wish to
warn my countrymen, travelling in Germany, against undue indulgence
in Liptauer cheese.

I am fond of cheese, and of trying new varieties of cheese; so that
when I looked down the cheese department of the bill of fare, and came
across "liptauer garnit," an article of diet I had never before heard of, I
determined to sample it.

It was not a tempting-looking cheese. It was an unhealthy, sad-
looking cheese. It looked like a cheese that had seen trouble. In
appearance it resembled putty more than anything else. It even
tasted like putty—at least, like I should imagine putty would taste.
To this hour I am not positive that it was not putty. The garnishing
was even more remarkable than the cheese. All the way round the
plate were piled articles that I had never before seen at a dinner, and
that I do not ever want to see there again. There was a little heap
of split-peas, three or four remarkably small potatoes—at least, I
suppose they were potatoes; if not, they were pea-nuts boiled soft,—
some caraway-seeds, a very young-looking fish, apparently of the
stickleback breed, and some red paint. It was quite a little dinner
all to itself.

What the red paint was for, I could not understand. B. thought that it was put there for suicidal purposes. His idea was that the customer, after eating all the other things in the plate, would wish he were dead, and that the restaurant people, knowing this, had thoughtfully provided him with red paint for one, so that he could poison himself off and get out of his misery.

I thought, after swallowing the first mouthful, that I would not eat any more of this cheese. Then it occurred to me that it was a pity to waste it after having ordered it, and, besides, I might get to like it before I had finished. The taste for most of the good things of this world has to be acquired. *I* can remember the time when I did not like beer.

So I mixed up everything on the plate all together—made a sort of salad of it, in fact—and ate it with a spoon. A more disagreeable dish I have never tasted since the days when I used to do Willie Evans's "dags," by walking twice through a sewer, and was subsequently, on returning home, promptly put to bed, and made to eat brimstone and treacle.

I felt very sad after dinner. All the things I have done in my life that I should not have done recurred to me with painful vividness. (There seemed to be a goodish number of them, too.) I thought of all the disappointments and reverses I had experienced during my career; of all the injustice that I had suffered, and of all the unkind things that had been said and done to me. I thought of all the people I had known who were now dead, and whom I should never see again, of all the girls that I had loved, who were now married to other fellows, while I did not even know their present addresses. I pondered upon our earthly existence, upon how hollow, false, and transient it is, and how full of sorrow. I mused upon the wickedness of the world and of everybody in it, and the general cussedness of all things.

I thought how foolish it was for B. and myself to be wasting our time, gadding about Europe in this silly way. What earthly enjoyment was there in travelling—being jolted about in stuffy trains, and overcharged at uncomfortable hotels?

B. was cheerful and frivolously inclined at the beginning of our walk (we were strolling down the Maximilian Strasse, after dinner); but as I talked to him, I was glad to notice that he gradually grew more serious and subdued. He is not really bad, you know, only thoughtless.

B. bought some cigars and offered me one. I did not want to smoke. Smoking seemed to me, just then, a foolish waste of time and money. As I said to B.:

"In a few more years, perhaps before this very month is gone, we shall be lying in the silent tomb, with the worms feeding on us. Of what advantage will it be to us then that we smoked these cigars to-day?"

B. said:

"Well, the advantage it will be to me now is, that if you have a cigar in your mouth I shan't get quite so much of your chatty conversation. Take one, for my sake."

To humour him, I lit up.

I do not admire the German cigar. B. says that when you consider they only cost a penny, you cannot grumble. But what I say is, that when you consider they are dear at six a half-penny, you can grumble. Well boiled, they might serve for greens; but as smoking material they are not worth the match with which you light them, especially not if the match be a German one. The German match is quite a high art work. It has a yellow head and a magenta or green stem, and can certainly lay claim to being the handsomest match in Europe.

We smoked a good many penny cigars during our stay in Germany, and that we were none the worse for doing so I consider as proof of our splendid physique and constitution. I think the German cigar test might, with reason, be adopted by life insurance offices.—Question: "Are you at present, and have you always been, of robust health?" Answer: "I have smoked a German cigar, and still live." Life accepted.

Towards three o'clock we worked our way round to the station, and began looking for our train. We hunted all over the place, but could not find it anywhere. The central station at Munich is an enormous building, and a perfect maze of passages and halls and corridors. It is much easier to lose oneself in it, than to find anything in it one may happen to want. Together and separately B. and I lost ourselves and each other some twenty-four times. For about half an hour we seemed to be doing nothing else but rushing up and down the station looking for each other, suddenly finding each other, and saying, "Why, where the dickens have you been? I have been hunting for you everywhere. Don't go away like that," and then immediately losing each other again.

And what was so extraordinary about the matter was that every time, after losing each other, we invariably met again—when we did meet—outside the door of the third-class refreshment room.

We came at length to regard the door of the third-class refreshment room as "home," and to feel a thrill of joy when, in the course of our weary wanderings through far-off waiting-rooms and lost-luggage bureaus and lamp depots, we saw its old familiar handle shining in the distance, and knew that there, beside it, we should find our loved and lost one.

When any very long time elapsed without our coming across it, we would go up to one of the officials, and ask to be directed to it.

"Please can you tell me," we would say, "the nearest way to the door of the third-class refreshment room?"

When three o'clock came, and still we had not found the 3.10 train, we became quite anxious about the poor thing, and made inquiries concerning it.

"The 3.10 train to Ober-Ammergau," they said. "Oh, we've not thought about that yet."

"Haven't thought about it!" we exclaimed indignantly. "Well, do for heaven's sake wake up a bit. It is 3.5 now!"

"Yes," they answered, "3.5 in the afternoon; the 3.10 is a night train. Don't you see it's printed in thick type? All the trains between six in the evening and six in the morning are printed in fat figures, and the day trains in thin. You have got plenty of time. Look around after supper."

I do believe I am the most unfortunate man at a time-table that ever was born. I do not think it can be stupidity; for if it were mere stupidity, I should occasionally, now and then when I was feeling well, not make a mistake. It must be fate.

If there is one train out of forty that goes on "Saturdays only" to some place I want to get to, that is the train I select to travel by on a Friday. On Saturday morning I get up at six, swallow a hasty breakfast, and rush off to catch a return train that goes on every day in the week "except Saturdays."

I go to London, Brighton and South Coast Railway-stations and clamour for South-Eastern trains. On Bank Holidays I forget it is Bank Holiday, and go and sit on draughty platforms for hours, waiting for trains that do not run on Bank Holidays.

To add to my misfortunes, I am the miserable possessor of a demon time-table that I cannot get rid of, a Bradshaw for August, 1887. Regularly, on the first of each month, I buy and bring home with me a new Bradshaw and a new A.B.C. What becomes of them after the second of the month, I do not know. After the second of the month, I never see either of them again. What their fate is, I can only guess. In their place is left, to mislead me, this wretched old 1887 corpse.

For three years I have been trying to escape from it, but it will not leave me.

I have thrown it out of the window, and it has fallen on people's heads, and those people have picked it up and smoothed it out, and brought it back to the house, and members of my family—"friends" they call themselves—people of my own flesh and blood—have thanked them and taken it in again!

I have kicked it into a dozen pieces, and kicked the pieces all the way downstairs and out into the garden, and persons—persons, mind you, who will not sew a button on the back of my shirt to save me from madness—have collected the pieces and stitched them carefully together, and made the book look as good as new, and put it back in my study!

It has acquired the secret of perpetual youth, has this time-table. Other time-tables that I buy become dissipated-looking wrecks in about a week. This book looks as fresh and new and clean as it did on the day when it first lured me into purchasing it. There is nothing about its appearance to suggest to the casual observer that it is not this month's Bradshaw. Its evident aim and object in life is to deceive people into the idea that it is this month's Bradshaw.

It is undermining my moral character, this book is. It is responsible for at least ten per cent. of the bad language that I use every year. It leads me into drink and gambling. I am continually finding myself with some three or four hours to wait at dismal provincial railway stations. I read all the advertisements on both platforms, and then I get wild and reckless, and plunge into the railway hotel and play billiards with the landlord for threes of Scotch.

I intend to have that Bradshaw put into my coffin with me when I am buried, so that I can show it to the recording angel and explain matters. I expect to obtain a discount of at least five-and-twenty per cent. off my bill of crimes for that Bradshaw.

The 3.10 train in the morning was, of course, too late for us. It would not get us to Ober-Ammergau until about 9 A.M. There was a train leaving at 7.30 (I let B. find out this) by which we might reach the village some time during the night, if only we could get a conveyance from Oberau, the nearest railway-station. Accordingly, we telegraphed to Cook's agent, who was at Ober-Ammergau (we all of us sneer at Mr. Cook and Mr. Gaze, and such-like gentlemen, who kindly conduct travellers that cannot conduct themselves properly, when we are at home; but I notice most of us appeal, on the quiet, to one or the other of them the moment we want to move abroad), to try and send a carriage to meet us by that train; and then went to an hotel, and turned into bed until it was time to start.

We had another grand railway-ride from Munich to Oberau. We passed by the beautiful lake of Starnberg just as the sun was setting and gilding with gold the little villages and pleasant villas that lie around its shores. It was in the lake of Starnberg, near the lordly pleasure-house that he had built for himself in that fair vale, that poor mad Ludwig, the late King of Bavaria, drowned himself. Poor King! Fate gave him everything calculated to make a man happy, excepting one thing, and that was the power of being happy. Fate has a mania for striking balances. I knew a little shoeblack once who used to follow his profession at the corner of Westminster Bridge. Fate gave him an average of sixpence a day to live upon and provide himself with luxuries; but she also gave him a power of enjoying that kept him jolly all day long. He could buy as much enjoyment for a penny as the average man could for a ten-pound note—more, I almost think. He did not know he was badly off, any more than King Ludwig knew he was well off; and all day long he laughed and played, and worked a little—not more than he could help—and ate and drank, and gambled. The last time I saw him was in St. Thomas's Hospital, into which he had got himself owing to his fatal passion for walking along outside the stone coping of Westminster Bridge. He thought it was "prime," being in the hospital, and told me that he was living like a fighting-cock, and that he did not mean to go out sooner than he could help. I asked him if he were not in pain, and he said "Yes," when he "thought about it."

Poor little chap! he only managed to live like a "fighting-cock" for three days more. Then he died, cheerful up to the last, so they told me, like the plucky little English game-cock he was. He could not have been more than twelve years old when he crowed his last. It had been a short life for him, but a very merry one.

Now, if only this little beggar and poor old Ludwig could have gone into partnership, and so have shared between them the shoeblack's power of enjoying and the king's stock of enjoyments, what a good thing it would have been for both of them—especially for King Ludwig. He would never have thought of drowning himself then—life would have been too delightful.

But that would not have suited Fate. She loves to laugh at men, and to make of life a paradox. To the one, she played ravishing strains, having first taken the precaution to make him stone-deaf. To the other, she piped a few poor notes on a cracked tin-whistle, and he thought it was music, and danced!

A few years later on, at the very same spot where King Ludwig threw back to the gods their gift of life, a pair of somewhat foolish young lovers ended their disappointments, and, finding they could not be wedded together in life, wedded themselves together in death. The story, duly reported in the newspapers as an item of foreign intelligence, read more like some old Rhine-legend than the record of a real occurrence in this prosaic nineteenth century.

He was a German Count, if I remember rightly, and, like most German Counts, had not much money; and her father, as fathers will when proposed to by impecunious would-be sons-in-law, refused his consent. The Count then went abroad to try and make, or at all events improve, his fortune. He went to America, and there he prospered. In a year or two he came back, tolerably rich—to find, however, that he was too late. His lady, persuaded of his death, had been urged into a marriage with a rich somebody else. In ordinary life, of course, the man would have contented himself with continuing to make love to the lady, leaving the rich somebody else to pay for her keep. This young couple, however, a little lighter headed, or a little deeper hearted than the most of us, whichever it may have been, and angry at the mocking laughter with which the air around them seemed filled, went down one stormy night together to the lake, and sobered droll Fate for an instant by turning her grim comedy into a somewhat grimmer tragedy.

Soon after losing sight of Starnberg's placid waters, we plunged into the gloom of the mountains, and began a long, winding climb among their hidden recesses. At times, shrieking as if in terror, we passed some ghostly hamlet, standing out white and silent in the moonlight against the shadowy hills; and, now and then, a dark, still lake, or mountain torrent whose foaming waters fell in a long white streak across the blackness of the night.

We passed by Murnau in the valley of the Dragon, a little town which possessed a Passion Play of its own in the olden times, and which, until a few years ago, when the railway-line was pushed forward to Partenkirchen, was the nearest station to Ober-Ammergau. It was a tolerably steep climb up the road from Murnau, over Mount Ettal, to

Ammergau—so steep, indeed, that one stout pilgrim not many years ago, died from the exertion while walking up. Sturdy-legged mountaineer and pulpy citizen both had to clamber up side by side, for no horses could do more than drag behind them the empty vehicle.

Every season, however, sees the European tourist more and more pampered, and the difficulties and consequent pleasure and interest of his journey more and more curtailed and spoilt. In a few years' time, he will be packed in cotton-wool in his own back-parlour, labelled for the place he wants to go to, and unpacked and taken out when he gets there. The railway now carries him round Mount Ettal to Oberau, from which little village a tolerably easy road, as mountain roadways go, of about four or five English miles takes him up to the valley of the Ammer.

It was midnight when our train landed us at Oberau station; but the place was far more busy and stirring than on ordinary occasions it is at mid-day. Crowds of tourists and pilgrims thronged the little hotel, wondering, as also did the landlord, where they were all going to sleep; and wondering still more, though this latter consideration evidently did not trouble their host, how they were going to get up to Ober-Ammergau in the morning in time for the play, which always begins at 8 A.M.

Some were engaging carriages at fabulous prices to call for them at five; and others, who could not secure carriages, and who had determined to walk, were instructing worried waiters to wake them at 2.30, and ordering breakfast for a quarter-past three sharp. (I had no idea there were such times in the morning!)

We were fortunate enough to find our land-lord, a worthy farmer, waiting for us with a tumble-down conveyance, in appearance something between a circus-chariot and a bath-chair, drawn by a couple of powerful-looking horses; and in this, after a spirited skirmish between our driver and a mob of twenty or so tourists, who pretended to mistake the affair for an omnibus, and who would have clambered into it and swamped it, we drove away.

Higher and higher we climbed, and grander and grander towered the frowning moon-bathed mountains round us, and chillier and chillier grew the air. For most of the way we crawled along, the horses tugging us from side to side of the steep road; but, wherever our coachman could vary the monotony of the pace by a stretch-gallop—as, for instance, down the precipitous descents that occasionally followed upon some extra long and toilsome ascent—he thoughtfully did so. At

JEROME K. JEROME

such times the drive became really quite exciting, and all our weariness was forgotten.

The steeper the descent, the faster, of course, we could go. The rougher the road, the more anxious the horses seemed to be to get over it quickly. During the gallop, B. and I enjoyed, in a condensed form, all the advantages usually derived from crossing the Channel on a stormy day, riding on a switchback railway, and being tossed in a blanket—a hard, nobbly blanket, full of nasty corners and sharp edges. I should never have thought that so many different sensations could have been obtained from one machine!

About half-way up we passed Ettal, at the entrance to the Valley of the Ammer. The great white temple, standing, surrounded by its little village, high up amid the mountain solitudes, is a famous place of pilgrimage among devout Catholics. Many hundreds of years ago, one of the early Bavarian kings built here a monastery as a shrine for a miraculous image of the Virgin that had been sent down to him from Heaven to help him when, in a foreign land, he had stood sore in need, encompassed by his enemies. Maybe the stout arms and hearts of his Bavarian friends were of some service in the crisis also; but the living helpers were forgotten. The old church and monastery, which latter was a sort of ancient Chelsea Hospital for decayed knights, was destroyed one terrible night some hundred and fifty years ago by a flash of lightning; but the wonder-working image was rescued unhurt, and may still be seen and worshipped beneath the dome of the present much less imposing church which has been reared upon the ruins of its ancestor.

The monastery, which was also rebuilt at the same time, now serves the more useful purpose of a brewery.

From Ettal the road is comparatively level, and, jolting swiftly over it, we soon reached Ober-Ammergau. Lights were passing to and fro behind the many windows of the square stone houses, and dark, strange-looking figures were moving about the streets, busy with preparations for the great business that would commence with the dawn.

We rattled noisily through the village, our driver roaring out "Good Night!" to everyone he passed in a voice sufficient to wake up everybody who might be sleeping within a mile, charged light-heartedly round half-a-dozen corners, trotted down the centre path of somebody's front garden, squeezed our way through a gate, and drew up at an open door, through which the streaming light poured out upon two tall, comely lasses, our host's daughters, who were standing waiting for us in the porch. They led us into a large, comfortably furnished room, where a tempting supper of hot veal-chops (they seem to live on veal in Germany) and white wine was standing ready. Under ordinary circumstances I should have been afraid that such a supper would cause me to be more eager for change and movement during the ensuing six hours than for sleep; but I felt that to-night it would take a dozen half-baked firebricks to keep me awake five seconds after I had got my head on the pillow—or what they call a pillow in Germany; and so, without hesitation, I made a very satisfactory meal.

After supper our host escorted us to our bedroom, an airy apartment adorned with various highly-coloured wood-carvings of a pious but somewhat ghastly character, calculated, I should say, to exercise a disturbing influence upon the night's rest of a nervous or sensitive person.

"Mind that we are called at proper time in the morning," said B. to the man. "We don't want to wake up at four o'clock in the afternoon and find that we have missed the play, after coming all this way to see it."

"Oh! that will be all right," answered the old fellow. "You won't get much chance of oversleeping yourself. We shall all be up and about, and the whole village stirring, before five; and besides, the band will be playing at six just beneath the window here, and the cannon on the Kofel goes off at—"

"Look here," I interrupted, "that won't do for me, you know. Don't you think that I am going to be woke up by mere riots outside the window, and brass-band contests, and earthquakes, and explosions, and those sort of things, because it can't be done that way. Somebody's got to come into this room and haul me out of bed, and sit down on the bed and see that I don't get into it again, and that I don't go to sleep on the floor. That will be the way to get me up to-morrow morning. Don't let's have any nonsense about stirring villages and guns and German bands. I know what all that will end in, my going back to England without seeing the show. I want to be roused in the morning, not lulled off to sleep again."

B. translated the essential portions of this speech to the man, and he laughed and promised upon his sacred word of honour that he would come up himself and have us both out; and as he was a stalwart and determined-looking man, I felt satisfied, and wished him "Good-night," and made haste to get off my boots before I fell asleep.

Tuesday, The 27th

A Pleasant Morning.—What can one Say about the Passion Play?—B. Lectures.—Unreliable Description of Ober-Ammergau.—Exaggerated Description of its Weather.—Possibly Untruthful Account of how the Passion Play came to be Played.—A Good Face.—The Cultured Schoolboy and his Ignorant Relations.

I am lying in bed, or, to speak more truthfully, I am sitting up on a green satin, lace-covered pillow, writing these notes. A green satin, lace-covered bed is on the floor beside me. It is about eleven o'clock in the morning. B. is sitting up in his bed a few feet off, smoking a pipe. We have just finished a light repast of—what do you think? you will never guess—coffee and rolls. We intend to put the week straight by stopping in bed all day, at all events until the evening. Two English ladies occupy the bedroom next to ours. They seem to have made up their minds to also stay upstairs all day. We can hear them walking about their room, muttering. They have been doing this for the last three-quarters of an hour. They seem troubled about something.

It is very pleasant here. An overflow performance is being given in the theatre to-day for the benefit of those people who could not gain admittance yesterday, and, through the open windows, we can hear the rhythmic chant of the chorus. Mellowed by the distance, the wailing cadence of the plaintive songs, mingled with the shrill Haydnistic strains of the orchestra, falls with a mournful sweetness on our ears.

We ourselves saw the play yesterday, and we are now discussing it. I am explaining to B. the difficulty I experience in writing an account of it for my diary. I tell him that I really do not know what to say about it.

He smokes for a while in silence, and then, taking the pipe from his lips, he says:

"Does it matter very much what you say about it?"

I find much relief in that thought. It at once lifts from my shoulders the oppressive feeling of responsibility that was weighing me down. After all, what does it matter what I say? What does it matter what any of us says about anything? Nobody takes much notice of it, luckily for everybody. This reflection must be of great comfort to editors and critics. A conscientious man who really felt that his words would carry weight and influence with them would be almost afraid to speak at all. It is the man who knows that it will not make an ounce of difference to anyone what he says, that can grow eloquent and vehement and positive. It will not make any difference to anybody or anything what I say about the Ober-Ammergau Passion Play. So I shall just say what I want to.

But what do I want to say? What can I say that has not been said, and said much better, already? (An author must always pretend to think that every other author writes better than he himself does. He does not really think so, you know, but it looks well to talk as though he did.) What can I say that the reader does not know, or that, not knowing, he cares to know? It is easy enough to talk about nothing, like I have been doing in this diary hitherto. It is when one is confronted with the task of writing about *some*thing, that one wishes one were a respectable well-to-do sweep—a sweep with a comfortable business of his own, and a pony—instead of an author.

B. says:

"Well, why not begin by describing Ober-Ammergau."

I say it has been described so often.

He says:

"So has the Oxford and Cambridge Boat Race and the Derby Day, but people go on describing them all the same, and apparently find other people to read their descriptions. Say that the little village, clustered round its mosque-domed church, nestles in the centre of a valley, surrounded by great fir-robed hills, which stand, with the cross-crowned Kofel for their chief, like stern, strong sentinels guarding its old-world peace from the din and clamour of the outer world. Describe how the square, whitewashed houses are sheltered beneath great overhanging gables, and are encircled by carved wooden balconies and verandahs, where, in the cool of the evening, peasant wood-carver and peasant farmer sit to smoke the long Bavarian pipe, and chat about the cattle and the Passion Play and village politics; and how, in gaudy colours above the porch, are painted glowing figures of saints and virgins and such-like good folk, which the rains have sadly mutilated, so that a legless angel on one side of the road looks dejectedly across at a headless Madonna on the other, while at an exposed corner some unfortunate saint, more cruelly dealt with by the weather than he ever was even by the heathen, has been deprived of everything that he could call his own, with the exception of half a head and a pair of extra-sized feet.

"Explain how all the houses are numbered according to the date they were built, so that number sixteen comes next to number forty-seven, and there is no number one because it has been pulled down. Tell how unsophisticated visitors, informed that their lodgings are at number fifty-three, go wandering for days and days round fifty-two, under the not unreasonable impression that their house must be next door, though, as a matter of fact, it is half a mile off at the other end of the village, and are discovered one sunny morning, sitting on the doorstep of number eighteen, singing pathetic snatches of nursery rhymes, and trying to plat their toes into door-mats, and are taken up and carried away screaming, to end their lives in the madhouse at Munich.

"Talk about the weather. People who have stayed here for any length of time tell me that it rains at Ober-Ammergau three days out of every four, the reason that it does not rain on the fourth day being that every fourth day is set apart for a deluge. They tell me, also, that while it will be pouring with rain just in the village the sun will be shining brightly all round about, and that the villagers, when the water begins to come in through their roofs, snatch up their children and hurry off to the nearest field, where they sit and wait until the storm is over."

"Do you believe them—the persons that you say tell you these tales?" I ask.

"Personally I do not," he replies. "I think people exaggerate to me because I look young and innocent, but no doubt there is a ground-work of truth in their statements. I have myself left Ober-Ammergau under a steady drenching rain, and found a cloudless sky the other side of the Kofel.

"Then," he continues, "you can comment upon the hardihood of the Bavarian peasant. How he or she walks about bare-headed and bare-footed through the fiercest showers, and seems to find the rain only pleasantly cooling. How, during the performance of the Passion Play, they act and sing and stand about upon the uncovered stage without taking the slightest notice of the downpour of water that is soaking their robes and running from their streaming hair, to make great pools upon the boards; and how the audience, in the cheaper, unroofed portion of the theatre, sit with equal stoicism, watching them, no one ever dreaming even of putting up an umbrella—or, if he does dream of doing so, experiencing a very rude awakening from the sticks of those behind."

B. stops to relight his pipe at this point, and I hear the two ladies in the next room fidgeting about and muttering worse than ever. It seems to me they are listening at the door (our room and theirs are connected by a door); I do wish that they would either get into bed again or else go downstairs. They worry me.

"And what shall I say after I have said all that?" I ask B. when at last he has started his pipe again.

"Oh! well, after that," he replies, "you can give the history of the Passion Play; how it came to be played."

"Oh, but so many people have done that already," I say again.

"So much the better for you," is his reply. Having previously heard precisely the same story from half a dozen other sources, the public will be tempted to believe you when you repeat the account. Tell them that during the thirty year's war a terrible plague (as if half a dozen different armies, marching up and down their country, fighting each other about the Lord only knows what, and living on them while doing it, was not plague enough) swept over Bavaria, devastating each town and hamlet. Of all the highland villages, Ober-Ammergau by means of a strictly enforced quarantine alone kept, for a while, the black foe at bay. No soul was allowed to leave the village; no living thing to enter it.

"But one dark night Caspar Schuchler, an inhabitant of Ober-Ammergau, who had been working in the plague-stricken neighbouring village of Eschenlohe, creeping low on his belly, passed the drowsy sentinels, and gained his home, and saw what for many a day he had been hungering for—a sight of his wife and bairns. It was a selfish act to do, and he and his fellow-villagers paid dearly for it. Three days after he had entered his house he and all his family lay dead, and the plague was raging through the valley, and nothing seemed able to stay its course.

"When human means fail, we feel it is only fair to give Heaven a chance. The good people who dwelt by the side of the Ammer vowed that, if the plague left them, they would, every ten years, perform a Passion Play. The celestial powers seem to have at once closed with this offer. The plague disappeared as if by magic, and every recurring tenth year since, the Ober-Ammergauites have kept their promise and played their Passion Play. They act it to this day as a pious observance. Before each performance all the characters gather together on the stage around their pastor, and, kneeling, pray for a blessing upon the work then about to commence. The profits that are made, after paying the performers a wage that just compensates them for their loss of time—wood-carver Maier, who plays the Christ, only receives about fifty pounds for the whole of the thirty or so performances given during the season, to say nothing of the winter's rehearsals—is put aside, part for the temporal benefit of the community, and the rest for the benefit of the Church. From burgomaster down to shepherd lad, from the Mary and the Jesus down to the meanest super, all work for the love of their religion, not for money. Each one feels that he is helping forward the cause of Christianity."

"And I could also speak," I add, "of grand old Daisenberger, the gentle, simple old priest, 'the father of the valley,' who now lies in silence among his children that he loved so well. It was he, you know, that shaped the rude burlesque of a coarser age into the impressive reverential drama that we saw yesterday. That is a portrait of him over the bed. What a plain, homely, good face it is! How pleasant, how helpful it is to come across a good face now and then! I do not mean a sainted face, suggestive of stained glass and marble tombs, but a rugged human face that has had the grit, and rain, and sunshine of life rubbed into it, and that has gained its expression, not by looking up with longing at the stars, but by looking down with eyes full of laughter and love at the human things around it."

"Yes," assented B. "You can put in that if you like. There is no harm in it. And then you can go on to speak of the play itself, and give your impressions concerning it. Never mind their being silly. They will be all the better for that. Silly remarks are generally more interesting than sensible ones."

"But what is the use of saying anything about it at all?" I urge. "The merest school-boy must know all about the Ober-Ammergau Passion Play by this time."

"What has that to do with you?" answers B. "You are not writing for cultured school-boys. You are writing for mere simple men and women. They will be glad of a little information on the subject, and then when the schoolboy comes home for his holiday they will be able, so far as this topic, at all events, is concerned, to converse with him on his own level and not appear stupid.

"Come," he says, kindly, trying to lead me on, "what did you think about it?"

"Well," I reply, after musing for a while, "I think that a play of eighteen acts and some forty scenes, which commences at eight o'clock in the morning, and continues, with an interval of an hour and a half for dinner, until six o'clock in the evening, is too long. I think the piece wants cutting. About a third of it is impressive and moving, and what the earnest student of the drama at home is for ever demanding that a play should be—namely, elevating; but I consider that the other two-thirds are tiresome."

"Quite so," answers B. "But then we must remember that the performance is not intended as an entertainment, but as a religious service. To criticise any part of it as uninteresting, is like saying that half the Bible might very well have been omitted, and that the whole story could have been told in a third of the space."

We talk on.—An Argument.—The Story that
Transformed the World.

A nd now, as to the right or wrong of the performance as a whole. Do you see any objection to the play from a religious point of view?"

"No," I reply, "I do not; nor do I understand how anybody else, and least of all a really believing Christian, can either. To argue as some do, that Christianity should be treated as a sacred mystery, is to argue against the whole scheme of Christianity. It was Christ himself that rent the veil of the Temple, and brought religion down into the streets and market-places of the world. Christ was a common man. He lived a common life, among common men and women. He died a common death. His own methods of teaching were what a Saturday reviewer, had he to deal with the case, would undoubtedly term vulgar. The roots of Christianity are planted deep down in the very soil of life, amid all that is commonplace, and mean, and petty, and everyday. Its strength lies in its simplicity, its homely humanness. It has spread itself through the world by speaking to the hearts, rather than to the heads of men. If it is still to live and grow, it must be helped along by such methods as these peasant players of Ober-Ammergau employ, not by high-class essays and the learned discussions of the cultured.

"The crowded audience that sat beside us in the theatre yesterday saw Christ of Nazareth nearer than any book, however inspired, could bring him to them; clearer than any words, however eloquent, could show him. They saw the sorrow of his patient face. They heard his deep tones calling to them. They saw him in the hour of his so-called triumph, wending his way through the narrow streets of Jerusalem, the multitude that thronged round him waving their branches of green palms and shouting loud hosannas.

"What a poor scene of triumph!—a poor-clad, pale-faced man, mounted upon the back of a shuffling, unwilling little grey donkey, passing slowly through the byways of a city, busy upon other things. Beside him, a little band of worn, anxious men, clad in thread-bare garments—fishermen, petty clerks, and the like; and, following, a noisy rabble, shouting, as crowds in all lands and in all times shout, and as dogs bark, they know not why—because others are shouting, or barking. And that scene marks the highest triumph won while he lived on earth by the village carpenter of Galilee, about whom the world has been fighting and thinking and talking so hard for the last eighteen hundred years.

"They saw him, angry and indignant, driving out the desecrators from the temple. They saw the rabble, who a few brief moments before had followed him, shouting 'Hosanna,' slinking away from him to shout with his foes.

"They saw the high priests in their robes of white, with the rabbis and doctors, all the great and learned in the land, sitting late into the night beneath the vaulted roof of the Sanhedrin's council-hall, plotting his death.

"They saw him supping with his disciples in the house of Simon. They saw poor, loving Mary Magdalen wash his feet with costly ointment, that might have been sold for three hundred pence, and the money given to the poor—'and us.' Judas was so thoughtful for the poor, so eager that other people should sell all they had, and give the money to the poor—'and us.' Methinks that, even in this nineteenth century, one can still hear from many a tub and platform the voice of Judas, complaining of all waste, and pleading for the poor—'and us.'

"They were present at the parting of Mary and Jesus by Bethany, and it will be many a day before the memory of that scene ceases to vibrate in their hearts. It is the scene that brings the humanness of the great tragedy most closely home to us. Jesus is going to face sorrow and death at Jerusalem. Mary's instinct tells her that this is so, and she pleads to him to stay.

"Poor Mary! To others he is the Christ, the Saviour of mankind, setting forth upon his mighty mission to redeem the world. To loving Mary Mother, he is her son: the baby she has suckled at her breast, the little one she has crooned to sleep upon her lap, whose little cheek has lain against her heart, whose little feet have made sweet music through the poor home at Bethany: he is her boy, her child; she would wrap her mother's arms around him and hold him safe against all the world, against even heaven itself.

"Never, in any human drama, have I witnessed a more moving scene than this. Never has the voice of any actress (and I have seen some of the greatest, if any great ones are living) stirred my heart as did the voice of Rosa Lang, the Burgomaster's daughter. It was not the voice of one woman, it was the voice of Motherdom, gathered together from all the world over.

"Oliver Wendell Holmes, in *The Autocrat of the Breakfast Table*, I think, confesses to having been bewitched at different times by two women's voices, and adds that both these voices belonged to German women. I am not surprised at either statement of the good doctor's. I am sure if a man did fall in love with a voice, he would find, on tracing it to its source, that it was the voice of some homely-looking German woman. I have never heard such exquisite soul-drawing music in my life, as I have more than once heard float from the lips of some sweet-faced German Fraulein when she opened her mouth to speak. The voice has been so pure, so clear, so deep, so full of soft caressing tenderness, so strong to comfort, so gentle to soothe, it has seemed like one of those harmonies musicians tell us that they dream of, but can never chain to earth.

"As I sat in the theatre, listening to the wondrous tones of this mountain peasant-woman, rising and falling like the murmur of a sea, filling the vast sky-covered building with their yearning notes, stirring like a great wind stirs Æolian strings, the thousands of trembling hearts around her, it seemed to me that I was indeed listening to the voice of the 'mother of the world,' of mother Nature herself.

"They saw him, as they had often seen him in pictures, sitting for the last time with his disciples at supper. But yesterday they saw him, not a mute, moveless figure, posed in conventional, meaningless attitude, but a living, loving man, sitting in fellowship with the dear friends that against all the world had believed in him, and had followed his poor fortunes, talking with them for the last sweet time, comforting them.

"They heard him bless the bread and wine that they themselves to this day take in remembrance of him.

"They saw his agony in the Garden of Gethsemane, the human shrinking from the cup of pain. They saw the false friend, Judas, betray him with a kiss. (Alas! poor Judas! He loved Jesus, in a way, like the rest did. It was only his fear of poverty that made him betray his Master. He was so poor—he wanted the money so badly! We cry out in horror against Judas. Let us pray rather that we are never tempted to do a shameful action for a few pieces of silver. The fear of poverty ever did, and ever will, make scamps of men. We would like to be faithful, and noble, and just, only really times are so bad that we cannot afford it! As Becky Sharp says, it is so easy to be good and noble on five thousand a year, so very hard to be it on the mere five. If Judas had only been a well-to-do man, he might have been Saint Judas this day, instead of cursed Judas. He was not bad. He had only one failing—the failing that makes the difference between a saint and a villain, all the world over—he was a coward; he was afraid of being poor.)

"They saw him, pale and silent, dragged now before the priests of his own countrymen, and now before the Roman Governor, while the voice of the people—the people who had cried 'Hosanna' to him—shouted 'Crucify him! crucify him!' They saw him bleeding from the crown of thorns. They saw him, still followed by the barking mob, sink beneath the burden of his cross. They saw the woman wipe the bloody sweat from off his face. They saw the last, long, silent look between the mother and the son, as, journeying upward to his death, he passed her in the narrow way through which he once had ridden in brief-lived triumph. They heard her low sob as she turned away, leaning on Mary Magdalen. They saw him nailed upon the cross between the thieves. They saw the blood start from his side. They heard his last cry to his God. They saw him rise victorious over death.

"Few believing Christians among the vast audience but must have passed out from that strange playhouse with their belief and love strengthened. The God of the Christian, for his sake, became a man, and lived and suffered and died as a man; and, as a man, living, suffering, dying among other men, he had that day seen him.

"The man of powerful imagination needs no aid from mimicry, however excellent, however reverent, to unroll before him in its simple grandeur the great tragedy on which the curtain fell at Calvary some eighteen and a half centuries ago.

"A cultivated mind needs no story of human suffering to win or hold it to a faith.

"But the imaginative and cultured are few and far between, and the peasants of Ober-Ammergau can plead, as their Master himself once pleaded, that they seek not to help the learned but the lowly.

"The unbeliever, also, passes out into the village street full of food for thought. The rude sermon preached in this hillside temple has shown to him, clearer than he could have seen before, the secret wherein lies the strength of Christianity; the reason why, of all the faiths that Nature has taught to her children to help them in their need, to satisfy the hunger of their souls, this faith, born by the Sea of Galilee, has spread the farthest over the world, and struck its note the deepest into human life. Not by his doctrines, not even by his promises, has Christ laid hold upon the hearts of men, but by the story of his life."

We Discuss the Performance.—A Marvellous Piece of
Workmanship.—The Adam Family.—Some Living Groups.—The
Chief Performers.—A Good Man, but a Bad Judas.—Where
the Histrionic Artist Grows Wild.—An Alarm!

And what do you think of the performance *as* a performance?" asks
B.

"Oh, as to that," I reply, "I think what everyone who has seen the play
must think, that it is a marvellous piece of workmanship.

"Experienced professional stage-managers, with all the tricks and
methods of the theatre at their fingers' ends, find it impossible, out
of a body of men and women born and bred in the atmosphere of the
playhouse, to construct a crowd that looks like anything else except a
nervous group of broken-down paupers waiting for soup.

"At Ober-Ammergau a few village priests and representative
householders, who have probably never, any one of them, been inside
the walls of a theatre in their lives, dealing with peasants who have
walked straight upon the stage from their carving benches and milking-
stools, produce swaying multitudes and clamouring mobs and dignified
assemblages, so natural and truthful, so realistic of the originals they
represent, that you feel you want to leap upon the stage and strangle
them.

"It shows that earnestness and effort can very easily overtake and pass
mere training and technical skill. The object of the Ober-Ammergau
'super' is, not to get outside and have a drink, but to help forward the
success of the drama.

"The groupings, both in the scenes of the play itself and in the various
tableaux that precede each act, are such as I doubt if any artist could
improve upon. The tableau showing the life of Adam and Eve after
their expulsion from Eden makes a beautiful picture. Father Adam,
stalwart and sunbrowned, clad in sheepskins, rests for a moment from
his delving, to wipe the sweat from his brow. Eve, still looking fair
and happy—though I suppose she ought not to,—sits spinning and
watching the children playing at 'helping father.' The chorus from each
side of the stage explained to us that this represented a scene of woe,
the result of sin; but it seemed to me that the Adam family were very

contented, and I found myself wondering, in my common, earthly way, whether, with a little trouble to draw them closer together, and some honest work to keep them from getting into mischief, Adam and Eve were not almost better off than they would have been mooning about Paradise with nothing to do but talk.

"In the tableau representing the return of the spies from Canaan, some four or five hundred men, women and children are most effectively massed. The feature of the foreground is the sample bunch of grapes, borne on the shoulders of two men, which the spies have brought back with them from the promised land. The sight of this bunch of grapes, we are told, astonished the children of Israel. I can quite understand its doing so. The picture of it used to astonish me, too, when *I* was a child.

"The scene of Christ's entry into Jerusalem surrounded by the welcoming multitude, is a wonderful reproduction of life and movement, and so also is the scene, towards the end, showing his last journey up to Calvary. All Jerusalem seems to have turned out to see him pass and to follow him, the many laughing, the few sad. The people fill the narrow streets to overflowing, and press round the spears of the Roman Guard.

"They throng the steps and balconies of every house, they strain to catch a sight of Christ above each other's heads. They leap up on each other's backs to gain a better vantage-ground from which to hurl their jeers at him. They jostle irreverently against their priests. Each individual man, woman, and child on the stage acts, and acts in perfect harmony with all the rest.

"Of the chief members of the cast—Maier, the gentle and yet kingly Christ; Burgomaster Lang, the stern, revengeful High Priest; his daughter Rosa, the sweet-faced, sweet-voiced Virgin; Rendl, the dignified, statesman-like Pilate; Peter Rendl, the beloved John, with the purest and most beautiful face I have ever seen upon a man; old Peter Hett, the rugged, loving, weak friend, Peter; Rutz, the leader of the chorus (no sinecure, his post); and Amalie Deschler, the Magdalen—it would be difficult to speak in terms of too high praise. Themselves mere peasants—There are those two women again, spying round our door; I am sure of it!" I exclaim, breaking off, and listening to the sounds that come from the next room. "I wish they would go downstairs; I am beginning to get quite nervous."

"Oh, I don't think we need worry," answers B. "They are quite old ladies, both of them. I met them on the stairs yesterday. I am sure they look harmless enough."

"Well, I don't know," I reply. "We are all by ourselves, you know. Nearly everyone in the village is at the theatre, I wish we had got a dog."

B. reassures me, however, and I continue:

"Themselves mere peasants," I repeat, "they represent some of the greatest figures in the world's history with as simple a dignity and as grand a bearing as could ever have been expected from the originals themselves. There must be a natural inborn nobility in the character of these highlanders. They could never assume or act that manner *au grand seigneur* with which they imbue their parts.

"The only character poorly played was that of Judas. The part of Judas is really *the* part of the piece, so far as acting is concerned; but the exemplary householder who essayed it seemed to have no knowledge or experience of the ways and methods of bad men. There seemed to be no side of his character sufficiently in sympathy with wickedness to enable him to understand and portray it. His amateur attempts at scoundrelism quite irritated me. It sounds conceited to say so, but I am convinced I could have given a much more truthful picture of the blackguard myself.

"'Dear, dear me,' I kept on saying under my breath, 'he is doing it all wrong. A downright unmitigated villain would never go on like that; he would do so and so, he would look like this, and speak like that, and act like the other. I know he would. My instinct tells me so.'

"This actor was evidently not acquainted with even the rudiments of knavery. I wanted to get up and instruct him in them. I felt that there were little subtleties of rascaldom, little touches of criminality, that I could have put that man up to, which would have transformed his Judas from woodenness into breathing life. As it was, with no one in the village apparently who was worth his salt as a felon to teach him, his performance was unconvincing, and Judas became a figure to laugh rather than to shudder at.

"With that exception, the whole company, from Maier down to the donkey, seemed to be fitted to their places like notes into a master's melody. It would appear as though, on the banks of the Ammer, the histrionic artist grew wild."

"They are real actors, all of them," murmurs B. enthusiastically, "the whole village full; and they all live happily together in one small valley, and never try to kill each other. It is marvellous!"

At this point, we hear a sharp knock at the door that separates the before-mentioned ladies' room from our own. We both start and turn pale, and then look at each other. B. is the first to recover his presence of mind. Eliminating, by a strong effort, all traces of nervousness from his voice, he calls out in a tone of wonderful coolness:

"Yes, what is it?"

"Are you in bed?" comes a voice from the other side of the door.

"Yes," answers B. "Why?"

"Oh! Sorry to disturb you, but we shall be so glad when you get up. We can't go downstairs without coming through your room. This is the only door. We have been waiting here for two hours, and our train goes at three."

Great Scott! So that is why the poor old souls have been hanging round the door, terrifying us out of our lives.

"All right, we'll be out in five minutes. So sorry. Why didn't you call out before?"

Friday, 30th, or Saturday, I Am Not Sure Which

TROUBLES OF A TOURIST AGENT.—HIS VIEWS ON TOURISTS.—THE
ENGLISH WOMAN ABROAD.—AND AT HOME.—THE UGLIEST
CATHEDRAL IN EUROPE.—OLD MASTERS AND NEW.—VICTUAL-
AND-DRINK-SCAPES.—THE GERMAN BAND.—A "BEER GARDEN."—
NOT THE WOMEN TO TURN A MAN'S HEAD.—DIFFICULTY OF
DINING TO MUSIC.—WHY ONE SHOULD KEEP ONE'S MUG SHUT.

I think myself it is Saturday. B. says it is only Friday; but I am positive
I have had three cold baths since we left Ober-Ammergau, which we
did on Wednesday morning. If it is only Friday, then I have had two
morning baths in one day. Anyhow, we shall know to-morrow by the
shops being open or shut.

We travelled from Oberau with a tourist agent, and he told us all his
troubles. It seems that a tourist agent is an ordinary human man, and
has feelings just like we have. This had never occurred to me before. I
told him so.

"No," he replied, "it never does occur to you tourists. You treat us as if
we were mere Providence, or even the Government itself. If all goes well,
you say, what is the good of us, contemptuously; and if things go wrong,
you say, what is the good of us, indignantly. I work sixteen hours a day to
fix things comfortably for you, and you cannot even look satisfied; while
if a train is late, or a hotel proprietor overcharges, you come and bully *me*
about it. If I see after you, you mutter that I am officious; and if I leave
you alone, you grumble that I am neglectful. You swoop down in your
hundreds upon a tiny village like Ober-Ammergau without ever letting
us know even that you are coming, and then threaten to write to the
Times because there is not a suite of apartments and a hot dinner waiting
ready for each of you.

"You want the best lodgings in the place, and then, when at a
tremendous cost of trouble, they have been obtained for you, you object
to pay the price asked for them. You all try and palm yourselves off for
dukes and duchesses, travelling in disguise. You have none of you ever
heard of a second-class railway carriage—didn't know that such things
were made. You want a first-class Pullman car reserved for each two
of you. Some of you have seen an omnibus in the distance, and have

JEROME K. JEROME

wondered what it was used for. To suggest that you should travel in such a plebeian conveyance, is to give you a shock that takes you two days to recover from. You expect a private carriage, with a footman in livery, to take you through the mountains. You, all of you, must have the most expensive places in the theatre. The eight-mark and six-mark places are every bit as good as the ten-mark seats, of which there are only a very limited number; but you are grossly insulted if it is hinted that you should sit in anything but the dearest chairs. If the villagers would only be sensible and charge you ten marks for the eight-mark places you would be happy; but they won't."

I must candidly confess that the English-speaking people one meets with on the Continent are, taken as a whole, a most disagreeable contingent. One hardly ever hears the English language spoken on the Continent, without hearing grumbling and sneering.

The women are the most objectionable. Foreigners undoubtedly see the very poorest specimens of the female kind we Anglo-Saxons have to show. The average female English or American tourist is rude and self-assertive, while, at the same time, ridiculously helpless and awkward. She is intensely selfish, and utterly inconsiderate of others; everlastingly complaining, and, in herself, drearily uninteresting. We travelled down in the omnibus from Ober-Ammergau with three perfect specimens of the species, accompanied by the usual miserable-looking man, who has had all the life talked out of him. They were grumbling the whole of the way at having been put to ride in an omnibus. It seemed that they had never been so insulted in their lives before, and they took care to let everybody in the vehicle know that they had paid for first-class, and that at home they kept their own carriage. They were also very indignant because the people at the house where they had lodged had offered to shake hands with them at parting. They did not come to Ober-Ammergau to be treated on terms of familiarity by German peasants, they said.

There are many women in the world who are in every way much better than angels. They are gentle and gracious, and generous and kind, and unselfish and good, in spite of temptations and trials to which mere angels are never subjected. And there are also many women in the world who, under the clothes, and not unfrequently under the title of a lady, wear the heart of an underbred snob. Having no natural dignity, they think to supply its place with arrogance. They mistake noisy bounce for self-possession, and supercilious rudeness as the sign of superiority.

They encourage themselves in sleepy stupidity under the impression that they are acquiring aristocratic "repose." They would appear to have studied "attitude" from the pages of the *London Journal*, coquetry from barmaids—the commoner class of barmaids, I mean—wit from three-act farces, and manners from the servants'-hall. To be gushingly fawning to those above them, and vulgarly insolent to everyone they consider below them, is their idea of the way to hold and improve their position, whatever it may be, in society; and to be brutally indifferent to the rights and feelings of everybody else in the world is, in their opinion, the hall-mark of gentle birth.

They are the women you see at private views, pushing themselves in front of everybody else, standing before the picture so that no one can get near it, and shouting out their silly opinions, which they evidently imagine to be brilliantly satirical remarks, in strident tones: the women who, in the stalls of the theatre, talk loudly all through the performance; and who, having arrived in the middle of the first act, and made as much disturbance as they know how, before settling down in their seats, ostentatiously get up and walk out before the piece is finished: the women who, at dinner-party and "At Home"—that cheapest and most deadly uninteresting of all deadly uninteresting social functions—(You know the receipt for a fashionable "At Home," don't you? Take five hundred people, two-thirds of whom do not know each other, and the other third of whom cordially dislike each other, pack them, on a hot day, into a room capable of accommodating forty, leave them there to bore one another to death for a couple of hours with drawing-room philosophy and second-hand scandal; then give them a cup of weak tea, and a piece of crumbly cake, without any plate to eat it on; or, if it is an evening affair, a glass of champagne of the you-don't-forget-you've-had-it-for-a-week brand, and a ham-sandwich, and put them out into the street again)—can do nothing but make spiteful remarks about everybody whose name and address they happen to know: the women who, in the penny 'bus (for, in her own country, the lady of the new school is wonderfully economical and business-like), spreads herself out over the seat, and, looking indignant when a tired little milliner gets in, would leave the poor girl standing with her bundle for an hour, rather than make room for her—the women who write to the papers to complain that chivalry is dead!

B., who has been looking over my shoulder while I have been writing the foregoing, after the manner of a *Family Herald* story-teller's wife in

JEROME K. JEROME

the last chapter (fancy a man having to write the story of his early life and adventures with his wife looking over his shoulder all the time! no wonder the tales lack incident), says that I have been living too much on sauerkraut and white wine; but I reply that if anything has tended to interfere for a space with the deep-seated love and admiration that, as a rule, I entertain for all man and woman-kind, it is his churches and picture-galleries.

We have seen enough churches and pictures since our return to Munich to last me for a very long while. I shall not go to church, when I get home again, more than twice a Sunday, for months to come.

The inhabitants of Munich boast that their Cathedral is the ugliest in Europe; and, judging from appearances, I am inclined to think that the claim must be admitted. Anyhow, if there be an uglier one, I hope I am feeling well and strong when I first catch sight of it.

As for pictures and sculptures, I am thoroughly tired of them. The greatest art critic living could not dislike pictures and sculptures more than I do at this moment. We began by spending a whole morning in each gallery. We examined each picture critically, and argued with each other about its "form" and "colour" and "treatment" and "perspective" and "texture" and "atmosphere." I generally said it was flat, and B. that it was out of drawing. A stranger overhearing our discussions would have imagined that we knew something about painting. We would stand in front of a canvas for ten minutes, drinking it in. We would walk round it, so as to get the proper light upon it and to better realise the artist's aim. We would back away from it on to the toes of the people behind, until we reached the correct "distance," and then sit down and shade our eyes, and criticise it from there; and then we would go up and put our noses against it, and examine the workmanship in detail.

This is how we used to look at pictures in the early stages of our Munich art studies. Now we use picture galleries to practise spurts in.

I did a hundred yards this morning through the old Pantechnicon in twenty-two and a half seconds, which, for fair heel-and-toe walking, I consider very creditable. B. took five-eighths of a second longer for the same distance; but then he dawdled to look at a Raphael.

The "Pantechnicon," I should explain, is the name we have, for our own purposes, given to what the Munichers prefer to call the Pinakothek. We could never pronounce Pinakothek properly. We called it "Pynniosec," "Pintactec," and the "Happy Tack." B. one day after dinner called it the "Penny Cock," and then we both got frightened, and agreed to fix up some sensible, practical name for it before any mischief was done. We finally decided on "Pantechnicon," which begins with a "P," and is a dignified, old-established name, and one that we can both pronounce. It is quite as long, and nearly as difficult to spell, before you know how, as the other, added to which it has a homely sound. It seemed to be the very word.

The old Pantechnicon is devoted to the works of the old masters; I shall not say anything about these, as I do not wish to disturb in any way the critical opinion that Europe has already formed concerning them. I prefer that the art schools of the world should judge for themselves in the matter. I will merely remark here, for purposes of reference, that I thought some of the pictures very beautiful, and that others I did not care for.

What struck me as most curious about the exhibition was the number of canvases dealing with food stuffs. Twenty-five per cent. of the pictures in the place seem to have been painted as advertisements for somebody's home-grown seeds, or as coloured supplements to be given away with the summer number of the leading gardening journal of the period.

"What could have induced these old fellows," I said to B., "to choose such very uninteresting subjects? Who on earth cares to look at the life-sized portrait of a cabbage and a peck of peas, or at these no doubt masterly representations of a cut from the joint with bread and vegetables? Look at that 'View in a ham-and-beef shop,' No. 7063, size sixty feet by forty. It must have taken the artist a couple of years to paint. Who did he expect was going to buy it? And that Christmas-hamper scene over in the corner; was it painted, do you think, by some poor, half-starved devil, who thought he would have something to eat in the house, if it were only a picture of it?"

B. said he thought that the explanation was that the ancient patrons of art were gentry with a very strong idea of the fitness of things. For "their churches and cathedrals," said B., "they had painted all those virgins and martyrs and over-fed angels that you see everywhere about Europe. For their bedrooms, they ordered those—well, those bedroom sort of pictures, that you may have noticed here and there; and then I expect they used these victual-and-drink-scapes for their banqueting halls. It must have been like a gin-and-bitters to them, the sight of all that food."

In the new Pantechnicon is exhibited the modern art of Germany. This appeared to me to be exceedingly poor stuff. It seemed to belong to the illustrated Christmas number school of art. It was good, sound, respectable work enough. There was plenty of colour about it, and you could tell what everything was meant for. But there seemed no imagination, no individuality, no thought, anywhere. Each picture looked as though it could have been produced by anyone who had studied and practised art for the requisite number of years, and who was not a born fool. At all events, this is my opinion; and, as I know nothing whatever about art, I speak without prejudice.

One thing I have enjoyed at Munich very much, and that has been the music. The German band that you hear in the square in London while you are trying to compose an essay on the civilising influence of music, is not the sort of band that you hear in Germany. The German bands that come to London are bands that have fled from Germany, in order to save their lives. In Germany, these bands would be slaughtered at the public expense and their bodies given to the poor for sausages. The bands that the Germans keep for themselves are magnificent bands.

Munich of all places in the now united Fatherland, has, I suppose, the greatest reputation for its military bands, and the citizens are allowed, not only to pay for them, but to hear them. Two or three times a day in different parts of the city one or another of them will be playing *pro bono publico*, and, in the evening, they are loaned out by the authorities to the proprietors of the big beer-gardens.

"Go" and dash are the chief characteristics of their method; but, when needed, they can produce from the battered, time-worn trumpets, which have been handed down from player to player since the regiment was first formed, notes as soft and full and clear as any that could start from the strings of some old violin.

The German band in Germany has to know its business to be listened to by a German audience. The Bavarian artisan or shopkeeper understands and appreciates good music, as he understands and appreciates good beer. You cannot impose upon him with an inferior article. A music-hall audience in Munich are very particular as to how their beloved Wagner is rendered, and the trifles from Mozart and Haydn that they love to take in with their sausages and salad, and which, when performed to their satisfaction, they will thunderously applaud, must not be taken liberties with, or they will know the reason why.

The German beer-garden should be visited by everyone who would see the German people as well as their churches and castles. It is here that the workers of all kinds congregate in the evening. Here, after the labours of the day, come the tradesman with his wife and family, the young clerk with his betrothed and—also her mother, alack and well-a-day!—the soldier with his sweetheart, the students in twos and threes, the little grisette with her cousin, the shop-boy and the workman.

Here come grey-haired Darby and Joan, and, over the mug of beer they share between them, they sit thinking of the children—of little Lisa, married to clever Karl, who is pushing his way in the far-off land that lies across the great sea; of laughing Elsie, settled in Hamburg, who has grandchildren of her own now; of fair-haired Franz, his mother's pet, who fell in sunny France, fighting for the fatherland. At the next table sits a blushing, happy little maid, full of haughty airs and graces, such as may be excused to a little maid who has just saved a no doubt promising, but at present somewhat awkward-looking, youth from lifelong misery, if not madness and suicide (depend upon it, that is the alternative he put before her), by at last condescending to give him the plump little hand, that he, thinking nobody sees him, holds so tightly beneath the table-cloth. Opposite, a family group sit discussing omelettes and a bottle of white wine. The father contented, good-humoured, and laughing; the small child grave and solemn, eating and drinking in business-like fashion; the mother smiling at both, yet not forgetting to eat.

I think one would learn to love these German women if one lived among them for long. There is something so sweet, so womanly, so genuine about them. They seem to shed around them, from their bright, good-tempered faces, a healthy atmosphere of all that is homely, and simple, and good. Looking into their quiet, steadfast eyes, one dreams of white household linen, folded in great presses; of sweet-smelling herbs; of savoury, appetising things being cooked for supper; of bright-polished furniture; of the patter of tiny feet; of little high-pitched voices, asking silly questions; of quiet talks in the lamp-lit parlour after the children are in bed, upon important questions of house management and home politics, while long stockings are being darned.

They are not the sort of women to turn a man's head, but they are the sort of women to lay hold of a man's heart—very gently at first, so that he hardly knows that they have touched it, and then, with soft, clinging tendrils that wrap themselves tighter and tighter year by year around it, and draw him closer and closer—till, as, one by one, the false visions and hot passions of his youth fade away, the plain homely figure fills more and more his days—till it grows to mean for him all the better, more lasting, true part of life—till he feels that the

JEROME K. JEROME

strong, gentle mother-nature that has stood so long beside him has been welded firmly into his own, and that they twain are now at last one finished whole.

We had our dinner at a beer-garden the day before yesterday. We thought it would be pleasant to eat and drink to the accompaniment of music, but we found that in practice this was not so. To dine successfully to music needs a very strong digestion—especially in Bavaria.

The band that performs at a Munich beer-garden is not the sort of band that can be ignored. The members of a Munich military band are big, broad-chested fellows, and they are not afraid of work. They do not talk much, and they never whistle. They keep all their breath to do their duty with. They do not blow their very hardest, for fear of bursting their instruments; but whatever pressure to the square inch the trumpet, cornet, or trombone, as the case may be, is calculated to be capable of sustaining without permanent injury (and they are tolerably sound and well-seasoned utensils), that pressure the conscientious German bandsman puts upon each square inch of the trumpet, cornet, or trombone, as the case may be.

If you are within a mile of a Munich military band, and are not stone deaf, you listen to it, and do not think of much else. It compels your attention by its mere noise; it dominates your whole being by its sheer strength. Your mind has to follow it as the feet of the little children followed the playing of the Pied Piper. Whatever you do, you have to do in unison with the band. All through our meal we had to keep time with the music.

We ate our soup to slow waltz time, with the result that every spoonful was cold before we got it up to our mouth. Just as the fish came, the band started a quick polka, and the consequence of that was that we had not time to pick out the bones. We gulped down white wine to the "Blacksmith's Galop," and if the tune had lasted much longer we should both have been blind drunk. With the advent of our steaks, the band struck up a selection from Wagner.

I know of no modern European composer so difficult to eat beefsteak to as Wagner. That we did not choke ourselves is a miracle. Wagner's orchestration is most trying to follow. We had to give up all idea of mustard. B. tried to eat a bit of bread with his steak, and got most hopelessly out of tune. I am afraid I was a little flat myself during the "Valkyries' Ride." My steak was rather underdone, and I could not work it quickly enough.

After getting outside hard beefsteak to Wagner, putting away potato salad to the garden music out of *Faust* was comparatively simple. Once or twice a slice of potato stuck in our throat during a very high note, but, on the whole, our rendering was fairly artistic.

We rattled off a sweet omelette to a symphony in G—or F, or else K; I won't be positive as to the precise letter; but it was something in the alphabet, I know—and bolted our cheese to the ballet music from *Carmen*. After which we rolled about in agonies to all the national airs of Europe.

If ever you visit a German beer-hall or garden—to study character or anything of that kind—be careful, when you have finished drinking your beer, to shut the cover of the mug down tight. If you leave it with the cover standing open, that is taken as a sign that you want more beer, and the girl snatches it away and brings it back refilled.

B. and I very nearly had an accident one warm night, owing to our ignorance of this custom. Each time after we had swallowed the quart, we left the pot, standing before us with the cover up, and each time it was, in consequence, taken away, and brought back to us, brimming full again. After about the sixth time, we gently remonstrated.

"This is very kind of you, my good girl," B. said, "but really I don't think we *can*. I don't think we ought to. You must not go on doing this sort of thing. We will drink this one now that you have brought it, but we really must insist on its being the last."

After about the tenth time we expostulated still more strongly.

"Now, you know what I told you four quarts ago!" remarked B., severely. "This can't go on for ever. Something serious will be happening. We are not used to your German school of drinking. We are only foreigners. In our own country we are considered rather swagger at this elbow-raising business, and for the credit of old England we have done our best. But now there must be an end to it. I simply decline to drink any more. No, do not press me. Not even another gallon!"

"But you both sit there with both your mugs open," replies the girl in an injured tone.

"What do you mean, 'we sit with our mugs open'?" asks B. "Can't we have our mugs open if we like?"

"Ah, yes," she explains pathetically; "but then I think you want more beer. Gentlemen always open their mugs when they want them filled with beer."

We kept our mugs shut after that.

JEROME K. JEROME

Monday, June 9th

A Long Chapter, but happily the Last.—The Pilgrims' Return.—A Deserted Town.—Heidelberg.—The Common, or Bed, Sheet, Considered as a Towel.—B. Grapples with a Continental Time Table.—An Untractable Train.—A Quick Run.—Trains that Start from Nowhere.—Trains that Arrive at Nowhere.—Trains that Don't Do Anything.— B. Goes Mad.—Railway Travelling in Germany.—B. is Taken Prisoner.—His Fortitude.—Advantages of Ignorance.—First Impressions of Germany and of the Germans.

We are at Ostend. Our pilgrimage has ended. We sail for Dover in three hours' time. The wind seems rather fresh, but they say that it will drop towards the evening. I hope they are not deceiving us.

We are disappointed with Ostend. We thought that Ostend would be gay and crowded. We thought that there would be bands and theatres and concerts, and busy table-d'hotes, and lively sands, and thronged parades, and pretty girls at Ostend.

I bought a stick and a new pair of boots at Brussels on purpose for Ostend.

There does not seem to be a living visitor in the place besides ourselves—nor a dead one either, that we can find. The shops are shut up, the houses are deserted, the casino is closed. Notice-boards are exhibited outside the hotels to the effect that the police have strict orders to take into custody anybody found trespassing upon or damaging the premises.

We found one restaurant which looked a little less like a morgue than did the other restaurants in the town, and rang the bell. After we had waited for about a quarter of an hour, an old woman answered the door, and asked us what we wanted. We said a steak and chipped potatoes for two, and a couple of lagers. She said would we call again in about a fortnight's time, when the family would be at home? She did not herself know where the things were kept.

We went down on to the sands this morning. We had not been walking up and down for more than half an hour before we came across the distinct imprint of a human foot. Someone must have been there this very day! We were a good deal alarmed. We could not imagine how he came there. The weather is too fine for shipwrecks, and it was not a part of the coast where any passing trader would be likely to land. Besides, if anyone has landed, where is he? We have been able to find no trace of him whatever. To this hour, we have never discovered who our strange visitant was.

It is a very mysterious affair, and I am glad we are going away.

We have been travelling about a good deal since we left Munich. We went first to Heidelberg. We arrived early in the morning at Heidelberg, after an all-night journey, and the first thing that the proprietor of the Royal suggested, on seeing us, was that we should have a bath. We consented to the operation, and were each shown into a little marble bath-room, in which I felt like a bit out of a picture by Alma Tadema.

The bath was very refreshing; but I should have enjoyed the whole thing much better if they had provided me with something more suitable to wipe upon than a thin linen sheet. The Germans hold very curious notions as to the needs and requirements of a wet man. I wish they would occasionally wash and bath themselves, and then they would, perhaps, obtain more practical ideas upon the subject. I have wiped upon a sheet in cases of emergency, and so I have upon a pair of socks; but there is no doubt that the proper thing is a towel. To dry oneself upon a sheet needs special training and unusual agility. A Nautch Girl or a Dancing Dervish would, no doubt, get through the performance with credit. They would twirl the sheet gracefully round their head, draw it lightly across their back, twist it in waving folds round their legs, wrap themselves for a moment in its whirling maze, and then lightly skip away from it, dry and smiling.

But that is not the manner in which the dripping, untaught Briton attempts to wipe himself upon a sheet. The method he adopts is, to clutch the sheet with both hands, lean up against the wall, and rub himself with it. In trying to get the thing round to the back of him, he drops half of it into the water, and from that moment the bathroom is not big enough to enable him to get away for an instant from that wet half. When he is wiping the front of himself with the dry half, the wet half climbs round behind, and, in a spirit of offensive familiarity, slaps him on the back. While he is stooping down rubbing his feet, it throws itself with delirious joy around his head, and he is black in the face before he can struggle away from its embrace. When he is least expecting anything of the kind, it flies round and gives him a playful flick upon some particularly tender part of his body that sends him

JEROME K. JEROME

springing with a yell ten feet up into the air. The great delight of the sheet, as a whole, is to trip him up whenever he attempts to move, so as to hear what he says when he sits down suddenly on the stone floor; and if it can throw him into the bath again just as he has finished wiping himself, it feels that life is worth living after all.

We spent two days at Heidelberg, climbing the wooded mountains that surround that pleasant little town, and that afford, from their restaurant or ruin-crowned summits, enchanting, far-stretching views, through which, with many a turn and twist, the distant Rhine and nearer Neckar wind; or strolling among the crumbling walls and arches of the grand, history-logged wreck that was once the noblest castle in all Germany.

We stood in awed admiration before the "Great Tun," which is the chief object of interest in Heidelberg. What there is of interest in the sight of a big beer-barrel it is difficult, in one's calmer moments, to understand; but the guide book says that it is a thing to be seen, and so all we tourists go and stand in a row and gape at it. We are a sheep-headed lot. If, by a printer's error, no mention were made in the guide book of the Colosseum, we should spend a month in Rome, and not think it worth going across the road to look at. If the guide book says we must by no means omit to pay a visit to some famous pincushion that contains eleven million pins, we travel five hundred miles on purpose to see it!

From Heidelberg we went to Darmstadt. We spent half-an-hour at Darmstadt. Why we ever thought of stopping longer there, I do not know. It is a pleasant enough town to live in, I should say; but utterly uninteresting to the stranger. After one walk round it, we made inquiries as to the next train out of it, and being informed that one was then on the point of starting, we tumbled into it and went to Bonn.

From Bonn (whence we made one or two Rhine excursions, and where we ascended twenty-eight "blessed steps" on our knees—the chapel people called them "blessed steps;" *we* didn't, after the first fourteen) we returned to Cologne. From Cologne we went to Brussels; from Brussels to Ghent (where we saw more famous pictures, and heard the mighty "Roland" ring "o'er lagoon and lake of sand"). From Ghent we went to Bruges (where I had the satisfaction of throwing a stone at the statue of Simon Stevin, who added to the miseries of my school-days, by inventing decimals), and from Bruges we came on here.

Finding out and arranging our trains has been a fearful work. I have left the whole business with B., and he has lost two stone over it. I used to think at one time that my own dear native Bradshaw was a sufficiently hard nut for the human intellect to crack; or, to transpose the simile, that Bradshaw was sufficient to crack an ordinary human nut. But dear old Bradshaw is an axiom in Euclid for stone-wall obviousness, compared with a through Continental time-table. Every morning B. has sat down with the book before him, and, grasping his head between his hands, has tried to understand it without going mad.

"Here we are," he has said. "This is the train that will do for us. Leaves Munich at 1.45; gets to Heidelberg at 4—just in time for a cup of tea."

"Gets to Heidelberg at 4?" I exclaim. "Does the whole distance in two and a quarter hours? Why, we were all night coming down!"

"Well, there you are," he says, pointing to the time-table. "Munich, depart 1.45; Heidelberg, arrive 4."

"Yes," I say, looking over his shoulder; "but don't you see the 4 is in thick type? That means 4 in the morning."

"Oh, ah, yes," he replies. "I never noticed that. Yes, of course. No! it can't be that either. Why, that would make the journey fourteen hours. It can't take fourteen hours. No, of course not. That's not meant for thick type, that 4. That's thin type got a little thick, that's all."

"Well, it can't be 4 this afternoon," I argue. "It must be 4 to-morrow afternoon! That's just what a German express train would like to do—take a whole day over a six hours' job!"

He puzzles for a while, and then breaks out with:

"Oh! I see it now. How stupid of me! That train that gets to Heidelberg at 4 comes from Berlin."

He seemed quite delighted with this discovery.

"What's the good of it to us, then?" I ask.

That depresses him.

"No, it is not much good, I'm afraid," he agrees. "It seems to go straight from Berlin to Heidelberg without stopping at Munich at all. Well then, where does the 1.45 go to? It must go somewhere."

Five minutes more elapse, and then he exclaims:

"Drat this 1.45! It doesn't seem to go anywhere. Munich depart 1.45, and that's all. It must go somewhere!"

Apparently, however, it does not. It seems to be a train that starts out from Munich at 1.45, and goes off on the loose. Possibly, it is a young, romantic train, fond of mystery. It won't say where it's going to. It probably does not even know itself. It goes off in search of adventure.

"I shall start off," it says to itself, "at 1.45 punctually, and just go on anyhow, without thinking about it, and see where I get to."

Or maybe it is a conceited, headstrong young train. It will not be guided or advised. The traffic superintendent wants it to go to St. Petersburg or to Paris. The old grey-headed station-master argues with it, and tries to persuade it to go to Constantinople, or even to Jerusalem if it likes that better—urges it to, at all events, make up its mind where it *is* going—warns it of the danger to young trains of having no fixed aim or object in life. Other people, asked to use their influence with it, have talked to it like a father, and have begged it, for their sakes, to go to Kamskatka, or Timbuctoo, or Jericho, according as they have thought best for it; and then, finding that it takes no notice of them, have got wild with it, and have told it to go to still more distant places.

But to all counsel and entreaty it has turned a deaf ear.

"You leave me alone," it has replied; "I know where I'm going to. Don't you worry yourself about me. You mind your own business, all of you. I don't want a lot of old fools telling me what to do. I know what I'm about."

What can be expected from such a train? The chances are that it comes to a bad end. I expect it is recognised afterwards, a broken-down, unloved, friendless, old train, wandering aimless and despised in some far-off country, musing with bitter regret upon the day when, full of foolish pride and ambition, it started from Munich, with its boiler nicely oiled, at 1.45.

B. abandons this 1.45 as hopeless and incorrigible, and continues his search.

"Hulloa! what's this?" he exclaims. "How will this do us? Leaves Munich at 4, gets to Heidelberg 4.15. That's quick work. Something wrong there. That won't do. You can't get from Munich to Heidelberg in a quarter of an hour. Oh! I see it. That 4 o'clock goes to Brussels, and then on to Heidelberg afterwards. Gets in there at 4.15 to-morrow, I suppose. I wonder why it goes round by Brussels, though? Then it seems to stop at Prague for ever so long. Oh, damn this timetable!"

Then he finds another train that starts at 2.15, and seems to be an ideal train. He gets quite enthusiastic over this train.

"This is the train for us, old man," he says. "This is a splendid train, really. It doesn't stop anywhere."

"Does it *get* anywhere?" I ask.

"Of course it gets somewhere," he replies indignantly. "It's an express! Munich," he murmurs, tracing its course through the timetable, "depart 2.15. First and second class only. Nuremberg? No; it doesn't stop at Nuremberg. Wurtzburg? No. Frankfort for Strasburg? No. Cologne, Antwerp, Calais? Well, where does it stop? Confound it! it must stop somewhere. Berlin, Paris, Brussels, Copenhagen? No. Upon my soul, this is another train that does not go anywhere! It starts from Munich at 2.15, and that's all. It doesn't do anything else."

It seems to be a habit of Munich trains to start off in this purposeless way. Apparently, their sole object is to get away from the town. They don't care where they go to; they don't care what becomes of them, so long as they escape from Munich.

"For heaven's sake," they say to themselves, "let us get away from this place. Don't let us bother about where we shall go; we can decide that when we are once fairly outside. Let's get out of Munich; that's the great thing."

B. begins to grow quite frightened. He says:

"We shall never be able to leave this city. There are no trains out of Munich at all. It's a plot to keep us here, that's what it is. We shall never be able to get away. We shall never see dear old England again!"

I try to cheer him up by suggesting that perhaps it is the custom in Bavaria to leave the destination of the train to the taste and fancy of the passengers. The railway authorities provide a train, and start it off at 2.15. It is immaterial to them where it goes to. That is a question for the passengers to decide among themselves. The passengers hire the train and take it away, and there is an end of the matter, so far as the railway people are concerned. If there is any difference of opinion between the passengers, owing to some of them wishing to go to Spain, while others want to get home to Russia, they, no doubt, settle the matter by tossing up.

B., however, refuses to entertain this theory, and says he wishes I would not talk so much when I see how harassed he is. That's all the thanks I get for trying to help him.

He worries along for another five minutes, and then he discovers a train that gets to Heidelberg all right, and appears to be in most respects a model train, the only thing that can be urged against it being that it does not start from anywhere.

It seems to drop into Heidelberg casually and then to stop there. One expects its sudden advent alarms the people at Heidelberg station.

They do not know what to make of it. The porter goes up to the station-master, and says:

"Beg pardon, sir, but there's a strange train in the station."

"Oh!" answers the station-master, surprised, "where did it come from?"

"Don't know," replies the man; "it doesn't seem to know itself."

"Dear me," says the station-master, "how very extraordinary! What does it want?"

"Doesn't seem to want anything particular," replies the other. "It's a curious sort of train. Seems to be a bit dotty, if you ask me."

"Um," muses the station-master, "it's a rum go. Well, I suppose we must let it stop here a bit now. We can hardly turn it out a night like this. Oh, let it make itself comfortable in the wood-shed till the morning, and then we will see if we can find its friends."

At last B. makes the discovery that to get to Heidelberg we must go to Darmstadt and take another train from there. This knowledge gives him renewed hope and strength, and he sets to work afresh—this time, to find trains from Munich to Darmstadt, and from Darmstadt to Heidelberg.

"Here we are," he cries, after a few minutes' hunting. "I've got it!" (He is of a buoyant disposition.) "This will be it. Leaves Munich 10, gets to Darmstadt 5.25. Leaves Darmstadt for Heidelberg 5.20, gets to—"

"That doesn't allow us much time for changing, does it?" I remark.

"No," he replies, growing thoughtful again. "No, that's awkward. If it were only the other way round, it would be all right, or it would do if our train got there five minutes before its time, and the other one was a little late in starting."

"Hardly safe to reckon on that," I suggest; and he agrees with me, and proceeds to look for some more fitable trains.

It would appear, however, that all the trains from Darmstadt to Heidelberg start just a few minutes before the trains from Munich arrive. It looks quite pointed, as though they tried to avoid us.

B.'s intellect generally gives way about this point, and he becomes simply drivelling. He discovers trains that run from Munich to Heidelberg in fourteen minutes, by way of Venice and Geneva, with half-an-hour's interval for breakfast at Rome. He rushes up and down the book in pursuit of demon expresses that arrive at their destinations forty-seven minutes before they start, and leave again before they get there. He finds out, all by himself, that the only way to get from South Germany to Paris is to go to Calais, and then take the boat to Moscow. Before he has done with the timetable, he doesn't know whether he is in Europe, Asia, Africa, or America, nor where he wants to get to, nor why he wants to go there.

Then I quietly, but firmly, take the book away from him, and dress him for going out; and we take our bags and walk to the station, and tell a porter that, "Please, we want to go to Heidelberg." And the porter takes us one by each hand, and leads us to a seat and tells us to sit there and be good, and that, when it is time, he will come and fetch us and put us in the train; and this he does.

That is my method of finding out how to get from one place to another. It is not as dignified, perhaps, as B.'s, but it is simpler and more efficacious.

It is slow work travelling in Germany. The German train does not hurry or excite itself over its work, and when it stops it likes to take a rest. When a German train draws up at a station, everybody gets out and has a walk. The engine-driver and the stoker cross over and knock at the station-master's door. The station-master comes out and greets them effusively, and then runs back into the house to tell his wife that they have come, and she bustles out and also welcomes them effusively, and the four stand chatting about old times and friends and the state of the crops. After a while, the engine-driver, during a pause in the conversation, looks at his watch, and says he is afraid he must be going, but the station-master's wife won't hear of it.

"Oh, you must stop and see the children," she says. "They will be home from school soon, and they'll be so disappointed if they hear you have been here and gone away again. Lizzie will never forgive you."

The engine-driver and the stoker laugh, and say that under those circumstances they suppose they must stop; and they do so.

Meanwhile the booking-clerk has introduced the guard to his sister, and such a very promising flirtation has been taking place behind the ticket-office door that it would not be surprising if wedding-bells were heard in the neighbourhood before long.

The second guard has gone down into the town to try and sell a dog, and the passengers stroll about the platform and smoke, or partake of a light meal in the refreshment-room—the poorer classes regaling themselves upon hot sausage, and the more dainty upon soup. When everybody appears to be sufficiently rested, a move onward is suggested by the engine-driver or the guard, and if all are agreeable to the proposal the train starts.

Tremendous excitement was caused during our journey between Heidelberg and Darmstadt by the discovery that we were travelling in an express train (they called it an "express:" it jogged along at the rate of twenty miles an hour when it could be got to move at all; most of its time it seemed to be half asleep) with slow-train tickets. The train was stopped at the next station and B. was marched off between two stern-looking gold-laced officials to explain the matter to a stern-looking gold-laced station-master, surrounded by three stern-looking gold-laced followers. The scene suggested a drum-head court-martial, and I could see that B. was nervous, though outwardly calm and brave. He shouted back a light-hearted adieu to me as he passed down the platform, and asked me, if the worst happened, to break it gently to his mother.

However, no harm came of it, and he returned to the carriage without a stain upon his character, he having made it clear to the satisfaction of the court—firstly, That he did not know that our tickets were only slow-train tickets; secondly, That he was not aware that we were not travelling by a slow train; and thirdly, That he was ready to pay the difference in the fares.

He blamed himself for having done this last, however, afterwards. He seemed to think that he could have avoided this expense by assuming ignorance of the German language. He said that two years ago, when he was travelling in Germany with three other men, the authorities came down upon them in much the same way for travelling first-class with second-class tickets.

Why they were doing this B. did not seem able to explain very clearly. He said that, if he recollected rightly, the guard had told them to get into a first-class, or else they had not had time to get into a second-class, or else they did not know they were not in a second-class. I must confess his explanation appeared to me to be somewhat lame.

Anyhow, there they were in a first-class carriage; and there was the collector at the door, looking indignantly at their second-class tickets, and waiting to hear what they had to say for themselves.

One of their party did not know much German, but what little he did know he was very proud of and liked to air; and this one argued the matter with the collector, and expressed himself in German so well that the collector understood and disbelieved every word he said.

He was also, on his part, able, with a little trouble, to understand what the collector said, which was that he must pay eighteen marks. And he had to.

As for the other three, two at all events of whom were excellent German scholars, they did not understand anything, and nobody could make them understand anything. The collector roared at them for about ten minutes, and they smiled pleasantly and said they wanted to go to Hanover. He went and fetched the station-master, and the station-master explained to them for another ten minutes that, if they did not pay eighteen shillings each, he should do the German equivalent for summonsing them; and they smiled and nodded, and told him that they wanted to go to Hanover. Then a very important-looking personage in a cocked-hat came up, and was very angry; and he and the station-master and the collector took it in turns to explain to B. and his two friends the state of the law on the matter.

They stormed and raged, and threatened and pleaded for a quarter of an hour or so, and then they got sick, and slammed the door, and went off, leaving the Government to lose the fifty-four marks.

We passed the German frontier on Wednesday, and have been in Belgium since.

I like the Germans. B. says I ought not to let them know this, because it will make them conceited; but I have no fear of such a result. I am sure they possess too much common-sense for their heads to be turned by praise, no matter from whom.

B. also says that I am displaying more energy than prudence in forming an opinion of a people merely from a few weeks' travel amongst them. But my experience is that first impressions are the most reliable.

At all events, in my case they are. I often arrive at quite sensible ideas and judgments, on the spur of the moment. It is when I stop to think that I become foolish.

Our first thoughts are the thoughts that are given to us; our second thoughts are the thoughts that we make for ourselves. I prefer to trust to the former.

The Germans are a big, square-shouldered, deep-chested race. They do not talk much, but look as though they thought. Like all big things, they are easy-going and good-tempered.

Anti-tobacconists, teetotallers, and such-like faddists, would fare badly in Germany. A German has no anti-nature notions as to its being wicked for him to enjoy his life, and still more criminal for him to let anybody else enjoy theirs. He likes his huge pipe, and he likes his mug of beer, and as these become empty he likes to have them filled again; and he likes to see other people like *their* pipe and *their* mug of beer. If you were to go dancing round a German, shrieking out entreaties to him to sign a pledge that he would never drink another drop of beer again as long as he lived, he would ask you to remember that you were talking to a man, not to a child or an imbecile, and he would probably impress the request upon you by boxing your ears for your impertinence. He can conduct himself sensibly without making an ass of himself. He can be "temperate" without tying bits of coloured ribbon all about himself to advertise the fact, and without rushing up and down the street waving a banner and yelling about it.

The German women are not beautiful, but they are lovable and sweet; and they are broad-breasted and broad-hipped, like the mothers of big sons should be. They do not seem to trouble themselves about their "rights," but appear to be very contented and happy even without votes. The men treat them with courtesy and tenderness, but with none of that exaggerated deference that one sees among more petticoat-ridden nations. The Germans are women lovers, not women worshippers; and they are not worried by any doubts as to which sex shall rule the State, and which stop at home and mind the children. The German women are not politicians and mayors and county councillors; they are housewives.

All classes of Germans are scrupulously polite to one another; but this is the result of mutual respect, not of snobbery. The tramcar conductor expects to be treated with precisely the same courtesy that he tenders. The Count raises his hat to the shopkeeper, and expects the shopkeeper to raise his hat to him.

The Germans are hearty eaters; but they are not, like the French, fussy and finicky over their food. Their stomach is not their God; and the cook, with his sauces and *pates* and *ragouts*, is not their High Priest. So long as the dish is wholesome, and there is sufficient of it, they are satisfied.

In the mere sensuous arts of painting and sculpture the Germans are poor, in the ennobling arts of literature and music they are great; and this fact provides a key to their character.

They are a simple, earnest, homely, genuine people. They do not laugh much; but when they do, they laugh deep down. They are slow, but so is a deep river. A placid look generally rests upon their heavy features; but sometimes they frown, and then they look somewhat grim.

A visit to Germany is a tonic to an Englishman. We English are always sneering at ourselves, and patriotism in England is regarded as a stamp of vulgarity. The Germans, on the other hand, believe in themselves, and respect themselves. The world for them is not played out. Their country to them is still the "Fatherland." They look straight before them like a people who see a great future in front of them, and are not afraid to go forward to fulfil it.

GOOD-BYE, SIR (OR MADAM)

A Note About the Author

Born Jerome Clapp, English author and humorist Jerome K. Jerome (1859–1927) later changed his last name to mirror his first. As a child, Jerome dreamed of a career in politics, but was forced to quit his studies and find a job at age thirteen after his father passed away. Jerome worked various jobs, including working on the railway, joining a traveling acting company for three years, and volunteering as an ambulance driver for the French army. In 1888, he married Georgina Marris, and had one stepchild from his wife's previous marriage. Jerome earned success with his comedic work, including his novel *Three Men in a Boat*.

A Note from the Publisher

Spanning many genres, from non-fiction essays to literature classics to children's books and lyric poetry, Mint Edition books showcase the master works of our time in a modern new package. The text is freshly typeset, is clean and easy to read, and features a new note about the author in each volume. Many books also include exclusive new introductory material. Every book boasts a striking new cover, which makes it as appropriate for collecting as it is for gift giving. Mint Edition books are only printed when a reader orders them, so natural resources are not wasted. We're proud that our books are never manufactured in excess and exist only in the exact quantity they need to be read and enjoyed. To learn more and view our library, go to minteditionbooks.com